GREATER SWISS MOUNTAIN DOG

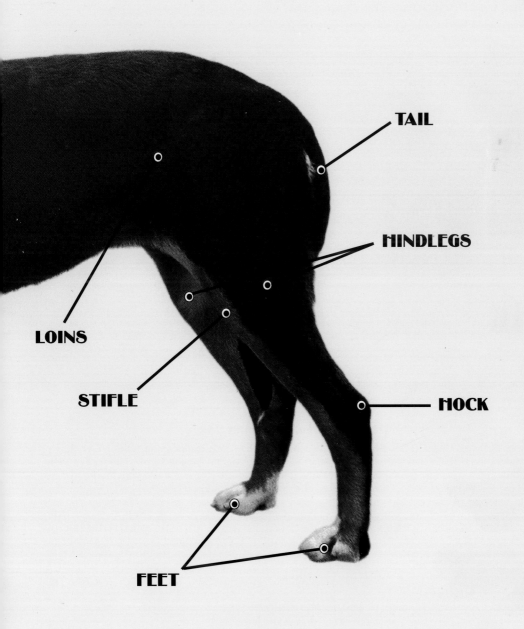

TAIL

HINDLEGS

LOINS

STIFLE

HOCK

FEET

Title Page: Saalbach Ashenda v. Pilch owned by Dan Campeau.

Photographers: Ashbey Photography, Cheri and Jim Barton, Mary Bloom, Kim Busch, Mary Jo Chieffe, the Christensen family, Donald and Diane Comp, Skip Conant, Colleen and Tim Darnell, Kathy Deyo, Isabelle Francais, Judy Iby, Kristin Kleeman, Joyce Kolkmann, Brian and Dawn Porto, Lori Price, Katherine Rynearson, Joel Spaeth, Nancy Sturgis, Julianne Wilson, Greg Witkop, Stanley Wotring.

Distributed in the UNITED STATES to the Pet Trade by T.F.H. Publications, Inc., One T.F.H. Plaza, Neptune City, NJ 07753; distributed in the UNITED STATES to the Bookstore and Library Trade by National Book Network, Inc. 4720 Boston Way, Lanham MD 20706; in CANADA to the Pet Trade by H & L Pet Supplies Inc., 27 Kingston Crescent, Kitchener, Ontario N2B 2T6; Rolf C. Hagen Inc., 3225 Sartelon St. Laurent-Montreal Quebec H4R 1E8; in CANADA to the Book Trade by Vanwell Publishing Ltd., 1 Northrup Crescent, St. Catharines, Ontario L2M 6P5 ; in ENGLAND by T.F.H. Publications, PO Box 15, Waterlooville PO7 6BQ; in AUSTRALIA AND THE SOUTH PACIFIC by T.F.H. (Australia), Pty. Ltd., Box 149, Brookvale 2100 N.S.W., Australia; in NEW ZEALAND by Brooklands Aquarium Ltd. 5 McGiven Drive, New Plymouth, RD1 New Zealand; in Japan by T.F.H. Publications, Japan—Jiro Tsuda, 10-12-3 Ohjidai, Sakura, Chiba 285, Japan; in SOUTH AFRICA by Lopis (Pty) Ltd., P.O. Box 39127, Booysens, 2016, Johannesburg, South Africa. Published by T.F.H. Publications, Inc.

MANUFACTURED IN THE
UNITED STATES OF AMERICA
BY T.F.H. PUBLICATIONS, INC.

GREATER SWISS MOUNTAIN DOG

A COMPLETE AND RELIABLE HANDBOOK

Jim Barton

RX-102

CONTENTS

mechanization of farming equipment and practices. It is also suspected that with the development of automotive transportation, particularly the invention of trucks, the need for a Swissy around the farm was merely aesthetic and no longer economical. Therefore, the need for the working Greater Swiss Mountain Dog declined in numbers in the rural agricultural regions of Switzerland. But it was not only farmers who used Swissys for the purpose of draft work. Many drawings and photographs from the late 1800s show the Greater Swiss Mountain Dog pulling carts, wagons and sleds. Small businesses found it much less expensive to keep and maintain a Swissy to pull wagons filled with their wares than a horse. It has been proposed that a Swissy can pull as much as a donkey with much less training required. Swissys needed no special housing arrangements, such as barns and paddocks, and a Swissy required less food.

Ten-week-old Barton Manor's Pure Karma owned by Lori Price taking his friends for a ride, keeping with the tradition of the Swissy as a draft dog.

As for their intelligence, folklore tells of the Swissy pulling a cart laden with milk and dairy products throughout a village without the presence of his owner. According to the story, the Swissy made all the correct stops then returned to his master only after completing the rounds.

The success of the Swissy as a draft dog led to the formation of clubs or societies for the promotion and improvement of draft regulations and for the protection and welfare of the dogs. Laws were enacted and enforced to ensure the safety of the draft dog throughout Europe. From this, competitions resulted to evaluate the agility, strength and speed that the draft dog possessed. These competitions continue today around the world in a variety of forms, in sled racing, weight pulling, freight pulling and carting competitions.

There is little written information about the history of the Greater Swiss Mountain Dog. However, according to the Greater Swiss Mountain Dog Club of America, Inc., "In 1908, quite by accident, a pure specimen was exhibited at a show in Langental. The Judge, Dr. Albert Heim of Zurich, was delighted with him and called him 'an example of the almost extinct Grosse Schweizer Sennenhund' (the Americanization of this

Although considered one of Switzerland's oldest breeds, the Greater Swiss Mountain Dog was not officially recognized by the AKC until 1995. Ch. Barton Manor's Diva owned by Nancy Sturgis.

Dropping in popularity after the mechanization of farming, the Greater Swiss thankfully was saved from virtual extinction by Swiss fanciers and careful breeding programs. Nox owned by Colleen and Tim Darnell.

title has resulted in the name Greater Swiss Mountain Dog), and urged breeders to save the few remaining specimens." This dog was entered in the Berner category at the show and Dr. Heim is further quoted as saying, "This dog belongs in a different category, he is too gorgeous and thoroughbred to push him aside as a poor example of a Berner." Upon his recommendation, several Swiss breeders began a careful breeding program to rescue the Greater Swiss Mountain Dog from virtual extinction.

In 1910, the Swiss Kennel Club officially recognized the Greater Swiss Mountain Dog as a breed and the first breed club was established. Along with this, the first breed standard was officially recognized. However, outside of these controlled breeding programs, very little information has been available concerning the Swissy anywhere in the Alpine Regions of Europe. What information is available is often sketchy and opinionated.

THE GREATER SWISS MOUNTAIN DOG IN AMERICA

In 1968 the first Swissy was imported into the United States by Patricia and Frederick Hoffman and

Perrin Rademacher. The Greater Swiss Mountain Dog Club of America, Inc. was formed with Mr. Rademacher as president and Mr. Hoffman as registrar. However, in my opinion, most of the credit for the quality of the Swissy being produced today rests with the late Dr. Howard and Mrs. Gretel Summons. They were in fact the mainstay breeders for the first 20 years of the breed in North America. Their conscientious effort to improve the structure, breeding stock and temperaments of the American Greater Swiss Mountain Dog positioned them as true mentors for the rest of us involved with this magnificent breed.

In recent years, American Swissys have been exported to Switzerland and other European countries as breeding stock. This is an obvious tribute to dedication of the Summons' efforts and diligence, as

The Greater Swiss Mountain Dog's origins as a farming dog are still evident today. Elsa Von Wumelsdorf owned by Johnathan K. Bastian.

well as that of the other American breeders who have established successful and conscientious breeding programs here in the United States.

Valuable information about the breed has been kept and continues to be maintained by the Greater Swiss Mountain Dog Club of America, Inc. A web page is available on the Internet for information about the breed and the club as well as club events. This site can be found at http://www.widomaker.com/gsmdca. Here you can find out more about the club, its activities and the locations of members and breeders near your area. If you are interested in becoming a member or finding out more about the club you can write to them at GSMDCA, PO Box 464, Burley, WA 98322.

DESCRIPTON OF THE GREATER SWISS MOUNTAIN DOG

The Greater Swiss Mountain Dog is considered by most to be the ideal family dog. Owners and breed clubs in this country, as well as throughout Europe, often further this claim. This title has not been "given" to the breed so much as it has been "earned" by the breed. Many stories abound of the Swissy's loyalty and faithfulness to their families. The one descriptor that is often quite unique to the Swissy, however, is that of the love the Swissy shows toward his human family. There are some who scoff at the idea that an animal is capable of love, but just look into the eyes of a Greater Swiss Mountain Dog as he watches his family and watch the expression on his face. And if you talk with a Swissy owner, you will soon find it evident that this love is not merely a one-sided emotion.

Over the years, I have personally observed the characteristics of the Greater Swiss Mountain Dog and heard many different stories about his fantastic interaction with the family, household pets, livestock and wildlife. If you have concerns about bringing such a large animal into a household that already has pets or to a farm with livestock, rest assured that the Swissy will interact with all in a highly admirable manner. Our Swissys live with an assortment of horses, ducks, geese and cats, as well as the neighbor's cattle. Equally so, the farm animals seem to like the presence of the Swissy. For example, over one particularly hard winter, foxes from the surrounding country side were killing our pond ducks. The surviving ducks quickly discovered that if they sat on the entry stoop to the Swissy's kennel, the foxes wouldn't bother them. They found that the Swissys offered them protection. As another example of the gentleness of the breed, I once had several of my Swissys lying next to my chair outside when several deer walked within 50 feet of us. The strongest reaction of the dogs was to each lift their head and give a muffled bark to let me know that the deer were there. The moment passed peacefully and the deer quietly moved on. In fact, when I feed my Swissys outside, I have to set out an extra bowl of food for our ducks. Otherwise the ducks chase the Swissys away from their food, and ducks are not known for aggressive behavior.

Many prospective buyers often suspect that Swissys, like some other large breeds, might have an excessive drooling characteristic. This is not the case with the Greater Swiss Mountain Dog. He is a dry-mouthed breed that has no excessive salivation. In a dog of this temperament, wanting to constantly be by your side as you stand or at your feet as you sit, this is a distinct advantage.

Unsolicited barking is fairly uncommon for the Greater Swiss Mountain Dog. Usually, you will find that your Swissy only barks when something out of the ordinary happens or when they are excited to see

The Greater Swiss is considered by many to be the ideal family dog because of his wonderful temperament and capacity to love. Nox shows his Swissy smile! Owners, Colleen and Tim Darnell.

The Swissy has an innate gentleness that he demonstrates with both people and animals. Ch. Snowy Mountain Alfred, owned by Matthew Zarrella, with his pet rooster.

you returning home from being out or during play. I recall shortly after becoming involved in the breed, I was awakened by my Swissys at three o'clock in the morning by their incessant barking. I reprimanded them numerous times until they finally quieted down, allowing me to fall back to sleep. The next morning as I drove down the lane to go to work, I saw my neighbor's barn had burned to the ground. I never doubted my Swissys again after that moment.

The "doggie odor" that is common to many breeds is also something you will not find on Greater Swiss Mountain Dogs. Their coat is not of an oily nature and their ears do not fall into their food or water as they eat. These characteristics, along with their dry mouths, all add to the fresh odor that is common to the Swissy.

Shedding is fairly light in comparison with many other more familiar breeds. As with other breeds of dog, daily brushing will remove loose hair that would otherwise fall out onto the floor. This brushing takes only minutes to accomplish. It also promotes healthy skin and coat, as well as allowing for moments of bonding between you and your Swissy. The coat is also of a texture that is softer, and therefore doesn't interweave itself into fabrics or carpeting, thus permitting ease in vacuuming and sweeping from flooring and upholstery. However, twice each year, in the spring and again in the autumn, the winter coat and summer coat respectively, will rapidly loosen and fall out. This is referred to as "blowing their coat" and usually only lasts for a couple weeks.

Swissys are generally long lived when compared to other large breed canines. It is not uncommon for a Swissy to live to be ten or twelve years old and there are records of many Swissys exceeding this age. The Swissy usually remains quite active and self sufficient throughout his life span.

If children are taught the proper way to handle a dog, they will always be comfortable around them. Annie and Jimmy Barton take a nap with a new litter.

In an effort to show the strength of the bonds between human and Swissy, I have included a letter I wrote a number of years ago when I was president of the Greater Swiss Mountain Dog Club of America as my "President's Message" in the Club's Newsletter.

As many of you know, my dog (GSMD Ch.) Ch. Lapp's Cranberry, CGC recently passed away. My family wishes to thank you all for your condolences during our time of grief.

It is so hard to believe because Bear never stopped eating, playing, or just being her happy self right up to the morning of her death. She had been to the vet for a brief check-up just two weeks prior and showed no sign of distress. But on Thursday morning she refused to eat and had difficulty walking. We checked her gums and found them very pale. I immediately took her to our vet who is only ten minutes away and he saw us as soon as we arrived. He suspected internal bleeding and started I. V. fluids and some other things to prevent Bear from going into shock. During this time I held her head in my arms and talked to her softly trying to comfort her. But throughout this whole process Bear watched me and kissed me gently trying to comfort me. As I look back, I now realize that she knew what was happening. During the final injection to sedate her before going into surgery I held her and told her how much she meant to me and she again kissed me back until she fell asleep. I find some comfort knowing that the last thing she heard was my voice telling her how much I loved her.

The operation revealed that her liver had ruptured due to cancer and was beyond repair. There was nothing anyone could do for her. We were all in a state of disbelief that this dog, who the night before was running and playing with the gang never showing any sign of distress or discomfort and who never missed a meal, was dying. She was euthanised, never regaining consciousness. I left the vet's office in somewhat a state of bewilderment.

Cheri brought Bear back to the farm to be buried. I picked out a favorite spot of hers where she used to lay and watch the happenings around the farm. My grief overwhelmed me several times as I dug her grave and I could see and hear my other Swissys sensing that something was seriously wrong. So when I finished digging I decided to get each of my dogs, the ones who were Bear's oldest buddies, and

Swissys are very protective, and the bond between a Swissy and his owner is a strong one. Rosie and Belle watch over Ryan Kleeman as he plays in the pool.

allowed them to say their goodbyes to her. I wasn't certain what to expect but I felt I owed it to them to have one last chance to see her. I was amazed and awed at what followed. Each had his or her unique way of approaching Bear's body but they were also alike in their humbled respect for her. Most silently sniffed and gently nudged at her, Wolfie lightly touched her shoulder a few times with his paw, Britta just stood there staring for what seemed an eternity, Leggy slowly circled Bear squealing over and over in a purely uninhibited display of remorse, Lappy lay down beside her as though she were guarding her or trying to keep her warm. After they each had these final moments with Bear they reluctantly returned to the house.

For many days afterward, I witnessed some of the most touching displays of canine respect and love for Bear. Over and over again, our Swissys visited her grave. Some would slowly return home only after being called repeatedly and others refused to leave unless I would go to them and gently coax them back.

It is my sincerest hope that each of you will spend a few extra quiet moments with your Swissys. Their time with us passes all too quickly.

My memory of Bear's life and now her death reminds me of quote from St. Francis. "Ask of the beasts and they shall teach you the beauty of the earth."

Although they look identical, every pup has his own personality and should be treated as an individual. A gang of Greater Swiss puppies bred by Jim and Cheri Barton.

Swissys are known for their seemingly unlimited patience and natural acceptance of children. Barton Manor's Renegade, owned by Suzanne and David Burbey and Cheri and Jim Barton, and his toddler friend.

INDIVIDUAL DIFFERENCES

The Greater Swiss Mountain Dog's personality can be as varied as the personalities of any group of animals. For example, in a collection of one hundred human beings we will find a multitude of individual characteristics unique to each individual; however, there will be many generalizations found common to the majority. The Greater Swiss Mountain Dog is no different in his uniqueness to the individual animal combined with an overall character common to the breed.

Nox is content to be where most Swissys can usually be found — under a pile of adoring kids! Owners, Colleen and Tim Darnell.

The Greater Swiss is naturally sensitive to the needs of all family members and has proven to be a wonderful therapy dog. Ch. Barton Manor's Diva owned by Nancy Sturgis.

Swissys are by nature non-aggressive when on lead or free running. However, the same dog in a crate, inside a fenced area or in an automobile will instinctively bark, lunge, jump and protect his "territory." But then again, immediately upon being let out of the enclosed area, this same Swissy should immediately calm to the demeanor of a self-assured, friendly Greater Swiss Mountain Dog. It is wise, however, to approach a Swissy, as any dog, with calm confidence and wait for the owner's permission to pet him.

It is often said that Swissys are wonderful around children, that a Swissy will naturally accept a child with a wagging tail and a Swissy smile. I find this to be very true. I can recall one of my bitches who would not leave my grandson alone while his mother was changing his diaper. She had to thoroughly examine the baby to ensure a satisfactory cleaning job before a new diaper was permitted to be placed back on the baby. I have found that Swissys naturally gravitate to children, wanting to play with them and explore the world with their new friend. Ask any Swissy owner who also has children and you will be treated to a multitude of wonderful stories about the adventures of the child/Swissy team.

I have noticed that Swissys rarely jump onto young children and usually give toddlers wide berth. However, that wagging tail can easily knock down a small toddler, and caution must be taken to avoid accidental injury to young children.

My experiences with Greater Swiss Mountain Dogs have revealed that they are also naturally sensitive to the elderly. Swissys often greet elderly individuals with reserved enthusiasm and naturally keep a substantial distance so as not to bump into them. Jumping and pouncing is usually done at a significant distance, again

Shamrock Klare, a therapy dog puppy, is being trained to work with children at school. Owner, Katherine Rynearson.

seemingly to avoid causing injury to the human. This reveals a natural characteristic that makes the Swissy ideal for therapy work with the elderly.

In therapy work, the Swissy quickly triggers sentiments within everyone they meet, which causes them to open up and communicate freely about their experiences when conversation might never occur otherwise. More often than not, conversations take place between the Swissy and the elderly, with the handler backing graciously away allowing this often deepest of communication to take place.

Swissys have the tendency to act like "big kids" and love to play and explore with their young friends. Sackett owned by Julianne Wilson with Sarah Liebert and Nathan Gilmore.

I can recall my first Swissy, Lapp's Anne (Lappy), as she visited a retirement home. She would gently nuzzle each person she met, laying her head on their laps if they were seated, awaiting the gentle pat on the head. On one occasion while visiting a bed-ridden patient, Lappy moved to the bed and lay her head on the bed next to the patient. After a moment, a paw slowly came to rest next to her head, then the other paw rose and came to rest. We immediately rose to remove Lappy but the attending nurse reprimanded us saying that this action had given the patient much pleasure and that Lappy was permitted to lay next to the patient. Lappy didn't need to be told twice, and she gently crawled into bed to lay next to the patient and remained there until visitation hours were over. This procedure followed throughout all her visitations.

Swissys don't stop there, however, they work their magic on their owners as well. The emotional stress we sometimes feel as we visit the elderly and ill is relieved by those big hugs that Swissys are so famous for. They hug us back as we hug them and they absorb the stress and melt it away, leaving us renewed and comforted.

If you would like to become active in therapy work, contact your local community social services department for the name and number of your nearest therapy dog organization. They will meet with you and your dog to evaluate and assist both of you for therapy dog work.

OFFICIAL STANDARD FOR THE GREATER SWISS MOUNTAIN DOG

General —The Greater Swiss Mountain Dog is a draft breed and should structurally appear as such. It is a striking, tri-colored, large, powerful dog of sturdy appearance.

Size, Proportion and Substance—Height at the highest point on the shoulder is ideally: Dogs 25 1/2 to 28 1/2 inches: Bitches—23 1/2 to 27 inches. Body length to height is a 10 to 9 proportion. The body is full.

Head—*Expression* is animated and gentle. The *eyes* are dark brown, medium sized, neither deep set nor prominent with closefitting eyelids. Eye rims are black. The *ears* are medium sized, set high, triangular

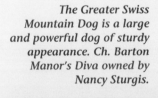

The Greater Swiss Mountain Dog is a large and powerful dog of sturdy appearance. Ch. Barton Manor's Diva owned by Nancy Sturgis.

in shape, gently rounded at the tip, and hang close to the head when in repose. When alert the ears are brought forward and raised at the base. The top of the ear is level with the top of the skull. The *skull* is flat and broad with a slight stop. The skull and muzzle are of equal length. The *muzzle* is blunt, not pointed. The muzzle is also strong and straight. The *nose* is always black. The *lips* are clean and as a dry-mouthed breed, flews are only slightly developed. The *teeth* meet in a scissor bite.

Neck, Topline and Body—The *neck* is of moderate length, strong, muscular and clean. The *topline* is level from the withers to the croup. The *chest* is deep and broad with a slight protruding breast bone. *Withers* are high and long. *Body* is full with a slight tuck-up. *Ribs* are well sprung. The *loins* are broad and strong. The *croup* is long, broad and smoothly rounded to the tail insertion. The *tail* is fairly level reaching to the hocks, carried down in repose and raised when excited. The bones of the tail should be straight.

Forequarters—The *shoulders* are long, sloping and strong. They are flat and well muscled. *Forelegs* are straight and strong. The *pasterns* slope very slightly, but are never weak. The *feet* are round and compact with well arched toes. The *dewclaws* may or may not be present.

Hindquarters—The *thighs* are broad, strong, and muscular. The *stifles* are moderately bent and taper smoothly into the hocks. The *hocks* are well let down and straight when viewed from the rear. *Dewclaws* must be removed. Feet are compact and turn neither in nor out.

The Greater Swiss is an alert and vigilant working dog. Shamrock Mercy v Schatz owned by Julianne Wilson.

Coat—The *top coat* is dense, 1 to 1 ½ inches long. The *undercoat* may be thick and sometimes showing.

Color—The *ground color* is jet black. The *markings* are rich rust and white. Symmetry of markings is desired. Rust appears over each eye, on each cheek and on each side of the chest, on all four legs, and under the tail. There is a white blaze and muzzle. A white marking on the chest typically forms an inverted cross. The tip of the tail is white, and white is present on the feet with rust between the white and black on each leg. White patches or a collar is permitted around the neck.

Gait—Good reach in front, powerful drive in rear. Movement with a level back.

Temperament—Bold, faithful, willing worker. Alert and vigilant. Nervousness or aggressiveness should be severely penalized.

Disqualifications

Any ground color other than black.

Blue eye color.

Approved: October 11, 1994

Effective: November 30, 1994

The Greater Swiss is a tri-colored dog with triangular ears, dark brown eyes and a gentle animated expression. Snowy Mt. Beaureguard Zuger owned by Glen and Lisa Simonsen.

BREED REQUIREMENTS

EXERCISE

Exercising the adult Swissy should involve moderation. If you are an avid jogger and want a dog to run along with you, the Greater Swiss is certainly not the companion. They are structurally suited for long walks, carrying backpacks or pulling burdens, not as a jogging animal. I strongly recommend against having Swissys run or jog for extended periods of time and distance.

Exercise should also be moderate for Swissy puppies. After all, Greater Swiss Mountain Dogs are working dogs and mature slowly. It will take approxi-

Built for endurance rather than speed, the Greater Swiss Mountain Dog should avoid heavy or extended periods of exercise. Owners, Glen and Lisa Simonsen.

Although appearing large in size, the Swissy puppy needs gentle handling until about three years of age when he is fully mature. Shamrock Hollis with Morag Miller.

mately three years for your Swissy to fully mature. Therefore, care must be taken not to assume that because he is a large dog, that he is mature at two years of age. Certainly the puppy should be encouraged to play and exercise; however, precautions must be taken not to permit rough play or rough handling by others.

Swissy puppies should NEVER be encouraged or allowed to jump up onto or from heights greater than the distance of an average step. This practice should continue through the first year. Jumping to or from heights can place shoulder and hip joints under great stress and can possibly result in damage to these body parts. It is therefore recommended that you should lift the puppy into vehicles or onto elevated

The Greater Swiss requires very little grooming and should be bathed only when absolutely necessary. Owner, Katie Carman.

areas. When he gets too large, lift the front two legs onto the object, then gently lift the hindquarters by the hind knees and place them so that firm footing is achieved by your puppy.

GROOMING

Greater Swiss Mountain Dog s are, as my wife puts it, "wash and wear dogs" — they are extremely easy to care for. I personally recommend bathing your Swissy only when absolutely necessary and then with baby shampoo. It's gentle on their skin and eyes and they smell nice and fresh afterward. A blow dryer and a towel are sufficient to thoroughly dry your Swissy in minutes.

A loyal and loving companion, the Greater Swiss Mountain Dog thrives when allowed to become an integral part of your family. The Kleeman family with all their pals.

COMPANIONSHIP

The Greater Swiss Mountain Dog needs and thrives on attention. It is imperative that you include him as an integral part of your family. He is a fantastically loyal companion to the entire family, as well as each individual within that family. Furthermore, unlike some breeds, the Swissy will readily accept new family members into your household. As long as you have properly socialized your Swissy from the day you brought him home, he will accept whomever you accept into your family unit.

Becoming well-socialized will allow your Swissy pup to interact with all kinds of people and animals. These two little guys are getting along just fine! Owner, Kim Busch.

Having a fairly large family of five children myself, each of our Swissys was individually introduced to our infants upon arriving from the hospital after delivery. Each and every Swissy sniffed the tiny person and looked up at us with that wide Swissy grin, showing their joy and acceptance.

If children are part of your family, you will quickly notice how Swissys bond to them genuinely enjoying the play and adventures children offer them. My children actually had our Swissys sliding down the playground slides as a routine part of their play.

SOCIALIZATION

When going for a walk, include your Swissy as part of any conversations you might have as you meet others along the way. This rapidly builds confidence in your pet and you will soon see a confident and well mannered Swissy. However, he must be discouraged from jumping on others or shying away from people he meets along the way.

As a Swissy matures, he inherently seems to key off his master, which allows him to know how to behave in various situations. For example, in a situation where you are walking your Swissy around the neighborhood, your Swissy will approach each individual you meet with a mannerism characteristic of your attitude toward that person.

As you approach individuals you are comfortable with but your Swissy does not recognize, you will observe that he will react from your manner and greet the strangers with ease. Individuals whom you might not know but are indifferent toward will be generally ignored by your Swissy. If someone approaches that makes you uneasy, you will observe your Swissy becoming cautious or protective of you, usually by walking between you and the stranger as they approach and pass you. Theory has it that the adrenaline that is excreted into our system during periods of excitement is exhaled and picked up by the dog's olfactory glands. This very well could be a factor triggering his behavior, but all signs suggest that your Swissy will react through visual observations of your actions and mannerisms.

A properly socialized Greater Swiss will adapt well to any surroundings and be a pleasure to be around. Barton Manor's King Hannibal owned by Suzanne and David Burbey.

SELECTING YOUR GREATER SWISS MOUNTAIN DOG

Making the choice to buy a Swissy is an easy one. The difficult part comes in deciding whether to buy a male or female, a companion or show-quality dog, a puppy or adult. These are not easy decisions. You will have to weigh all the options carefully so that both you and your new family member will benefit.

The decision to get a Greater Swiss should be carefully thought out by every member of the family. Alli Wade with four-month-old Nox owned by Colleen and Tim Darnell.

Equally important is the fact that a few breeders are in competition, in the show ring as well as for puppy sales and prestige. This can be found in any breed of dog. Therefore, when talking with breeders, it is important to recognize hearsay and innuendo and take it with a bit more than a grain of salt.

LOCATING A BREEDER

The Greater Swiss Mountain Dog Club of America offers a free breeder referral service to interested parties.

This service can recommend reputable breeders who are members of the national organization and who abide by the club's breeding principles. They will refer you to breeders who presently have litters available, as well as those breeders located in your area who you might wish to contact for further information about the breed or when future litters are planned.

It is always preferable to visit the breeder when possible in order to meet the sire and dam. This is important because the genetic code passed to your puppy will be a combination of both parents. You should study the physical quality of the parents, comparing their characteristics with those of the breed standard. Also, thoroughly examine the temperament of the parents. The bitch will be somewhat protective of her puppies, so it would be best to study how she reacts to her owners and their family members when with the puppies. However, when away from the puppies the dam should be friendly and approach you willingly and eagerly when you call her. If the sire is on the premises, you should be permitted to see him and allowed to interact with him. Shy, fearful or aggressive behavior toward you should send up a red flag that you should look elsewhere. Finally, examine a copy of the pedigree of both parents noting how closely related ancestors might be and titles earned. Take into consideration that there is a relatively small number of Greater Swiss Mountain Dogs of breeding quality in North America as well as in Europe, which results in a limited gene pool. Therefore, to some degree, ancestry might prove to be slightly similar on the

So many to choose from! When buying a Swissy, be sure to pick a reputable breeder that is concerned with preserving the qualities of the breed. Amy and Tabitha with puppies bred by Norman and DeLena Christensen.

It is advisable to confirm the absence of any genetic health problems in family lines of the litter you are considering. Owners, the Kleeman family.

grandparent and great-grandparent sides of the sire and dam of your prospective puppy.

Even though titles on the parents might seem unimportant because you have little or no interest in showing, it is, however, valuable information. The show dog is often subjected to many stressful situations, with all the training, preparation, traveling to the shows, staying in unfamiliar and uncomfortable environments, performing in just about any weather condition, going into a show ring with dogs he doesn't know, having strangers (judges) thoroughly examine them, being approached by the throngs of show enthusiasts who want to pet them outside the ring and then, finally, traveling back home. For any dog to accomplish these tasks and win titles on top of it says much for the temperament, appearance and structural superiority in the ancestry of your prospective puppy. It is wise to become familiar with the various titles that dogs might earn so as to know what all those prefixes and suffixes mean on their registry.

It is also advisable to ask if either the sire or dam have hip certification from one of the national registries like the Orthopedic Foundation for Animals (OFA). Some breeders have hip evaluations, front shoulder evaluations and eye evaluations on their dogs. This, of course, is no guarantee that your puppy will be free of these problems, but it can be to your puppy's advantage if either or preferably both parents are "clear" of any defects.

COMPANION OR SHOW?

Just as brothers and sisters are alike yet different, puppies in a litter are similar but also unique. Often times, it is an imperfection in color balance or markings, an incorrect bite, a knot or lump in the tail, a curled tail, extra eyelashes or some other quality that separates puppies into companion or show classification. Consider

35

Before deciding on a puppy or an adult, you must consider your family's needs and lifestyle. Meghan Chieffe with four-month-old Shamrock Helvita Engel. Owners, the Chieffe family.

what limitations of your new puppy you are willing to accept prior to selecting him or her.

"Do I want a companion or show Swissy?" This is often times a much more difficult decision than it initially seems because both have their merits. Both make excellent companions, but if you think you might eventually want to show your dog in conformation or have a litter of puppies, the show dog is your only choice. The initial decision is made many times on expense with the companion dog usually being less expensive. One additional expense to consider if you decide on a companion, however, is that responsible breeders require all pets to be spayed or neutered. This is also recommended by the Greater Swiss Mountain Dog Club of America, Inc., in order to prevent unwanted litters as well as ensuring that only the best specimens of Swissys will pass on the most favorable traits to their offspring.

MALE OR FEMALE?

Just about everyone has a personal preference as to whether a dog or a bitch makes the best companion or investment. Your primary concerns in picking your puppy should be with the parents temperaments; if they are both gentle, friendly and good natured, the puppies will probably be the same, regardless of sex.

Females are generally smaller in size and have less tendency to roam. Males on the other hand are larger and might occasionally roam, especially if they get the scent of a neighboring female in estrus. However, temperaments are quite similar, both being loyal, affectionate and alert.

PUPPY OR ADULT?

It is an enjoyable experience watching your puppy grow and mature into an adult dog. Your puppy will give you years of enjoyment and memories. You will be able to mold both your puppy's and your own personalities, habits and time schedules to fit each other. Raising your puppy will certainly be time consuming and at times even nerve racking, but it will also be a time of growth for both of you.

Some of us have busy lifestyles that while are conducive for owning a dog, do not allow the needed time for properly raising, housebreaking and training a puppy. Therefore, for some it might be to their advantage to purchase an older dog that is already trained. Also, for those interested in breeding, a mature bitch that has

If you wish to show your Greater Swiss Mountain Dog, you must pick a puppy that closely adheres to the breed standard. Ch. Shamrock Elliot v Sarmac owned by Julianne Wilson takes the prize.

already successfully produced a litter might be a wise investment. However, one must ask themselves and the owner why they would wish to sell a productive bitch with the potential for producing more litters. Keep in mind, however, that situations do arise where this does on occasion happen and a perfectly fine, productive bitch becomes available.

However, I personally recommend against a first time dog owner choosing the older dog. This option should be left to those with experience who know how to handle the mature dog's disposition. It is reasonable to assume that an older dog being given up for sale might, and I emphasize might, have some condition causing him to be given up or that the dog could possibly go through a period of depression at having to leave the only home he remembers for strange surroundings. Therefore, it is recommended that caution be taken when selecting an older dog of any breed.

CONCERNS OF THE GREATER SWISS

The one question that is debated, argued and studied the most concerning the Greater Swiss Mountain Dog is that of health concerns. In order to avoid hearsay and third person information, I will base my information on clinically diagnosed conditions of the Swissy.

BLOAT
The first and foremost concern with the Greater Swiss Mountain Dog is that of bloat, or gastric dilatation-volvulus. This is a disease or digestive problem that is of serious concern for most large and giant breed dog owners. Although I have seen where

Although a generally healthy breed, there are some specific health problems that are inherent in the Greater Swiss Mountain Dog. Jimmy Barton with his first patient.

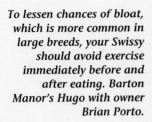

To lessen chances of bloat, which is more common in large breeds, your Swissy should avoid exercise immediately before and after eating. Barton Manor's Hugo with owner Brian Porto.

smaller dogs have been inflicted with this problem it remains more common in larger breeds. Bloat is a condition that most commonly affects dogs between the ages of three and seven years of age. However, younger and older dogs alike have been diagnosed with this condition. Bloat has and is being studied around the world by nearly every major veterinary university and institution. The cause is as elusive as any illness affecting man or beast, and therefore prevention is equally frustrating.

Canine bloat is the condition that is often fatal to affected dogs, therefore prompt medical attention is imperative. Signs of this condition might include:

1. Uneasiness, where the dog cannot relax or get comfortable.

2. Unsuccessful attempts at vomiting.

3. Enlarged abdomen, possibly hard to the touch.

4. Pale gums.

Delays of even minutes can make all the difference in the world. Therefore, contact your veterinarian or emergency veterinary medical clinic immediately for advice or better yet rush your dog to the office without delay. Ask your veterinarian for information and literature on this affliction so that you will be well prepared in the event of an emergency.

Following the suggested feeding instructions in this book as previously noted, canine bloat might be avoided. I have always recommended to new Swissy owners that they feed their puppies and adult dogs soaked kibble at least twice each day and never to radically change their diet at any point in their lives. Any and all dietary changes must be fazed in over a period of several days. Exercise should be avoided one hour before and two hours after feeding. Although fresh water must be available for your Swissy continually, the amount should be limited immediately after feeding.

HIP DYSPLASIA

Another condition that affects Swissys is hip dysplasia. Hip dysplasia is a condition where the ball and socket of the hips are not formed or seated properly. This could be very mild, and the dog will never have physical discomfort or movement disorders, or could become extreme, and hip replacement or other radical surgical procedures might be recommended. The severe cases usually result in crippling conditions for the dog as it matures.

EPILEPSY

Epilepsy is another condition occasionally found in the Swissy. There can be a breed predisposition to this malady; however, other environmental factors such as distemper, toxoplasmosis, lead poisoning and severe intestinal parasitism can also cause seizures. It is therefore prudent that sires and dams be free of this disorder and that puppies be maintained in such a fashion as to avoid environmental risks.

OSTEOCHONDROSIS

Osteochondrosis (OCD) is a condition classified as a secondary degenerative joint disease that is occasionally found in large and giant breeds. In Greater Swiss Mountain Dogs, this might be observed par-

Because he is a large breed, the Greater Swiss may be prone to certain joint diseases. Barton Manor's Hugo is just resting his bones. Owners, Brian and Dawn Porto.

Your Swissy's eyes should be clear and dark and any redness or irritation should be reported to your veterinarian. Jingle owned by the Kleeman family.

ticularly in the front shoulders. It particularly affects younger dogs between the ages of six to twelve months. There is some evidence of a genetic predisposition as well as environmentally caused factors. Therefore you should inquire as to whether either parents or siblings have ever had this disease. Also, follow your breeders recommendations on exercise and nutritional intake.

EYE PROBLEMS

Eye problems affecting the Greater Swiss Mountain Dogs range from distichiasis to entropion. In the case of distichiasis, abnormally positioned eye lashes along the eyelid margin may irritate the cornea. Distichiasis is common to all breeds of dogs and in most cases does not require medical treatment. Entropion, however, is a condition where the eyelid margin actually rolls inward to some extent. This could result in multiple eyelashes contacting the corneal surface causing irritation and eventually corneal ulceration. In both cases, veterinary care may be required to alleviate serious problems. Obviously, the few extra lashes of distichiasis usually requires minimal, if any, eye invasion or surgery whereas entropion may require extensive surgical procedures.

As a whole, you will find that when compared with other purebred canines, the Greater Swiss Mountain Dog is quite healthy and sound.

YOUR PUPPY'S NEW HOME

Before actually collecting your puppy, it is better that you purchase the basic items you will need in advance of the pup's arrival date. This allows you more opportunity to shop around and ensure you have exactly what you want rather than having to buy lesser quality in a hurry.

It is always better to collect the puppy as early in the day as possible. In most instances this will mean that the puppy has a few hours with your family before it is time to retire for his first night's sleep away from his former home.

If the breeder is local, then you may not need any form of box to place the puppy in when you bring him home. A member of the family can hold the pup in his lap—duly protected by some towels just in case the puppy becomes car sick! Be sure to advise the breeder at what time you hope to arrive for the puppy, as this will obviously influence the feeding of the pup that morning or afternoon. If you arrive early in the day, then they will likely only give the pup a light breakfast so as to reduce the risk of travel sickness.

A puppy is extremely vunerable and will depend on you, his owner, to take care of all his needs. Owners, Brian and Dawn Porto.

If the trip will be of a few hours duration, you should take a travel crate with you. The crate will provide your pup with a safe place to lie down and rest during the trip. During the trip, the puppy will no doubt wish to relieve his bowels, so you will have to make a few stops. On a long journey you may need a rest yourself, and can take the opportunity to let the puppy get some fresh air. However, do not let the puppy walk where there may have been a lot of other dogs because he might pick up an infection. Also, if he relieves his bowels at such a time, do not just leave the feces where they were dropped. This is the height of irresponsibility. It has resulted in many public parks and other places actually banning dogs. You can purchase poop-scoops from your pet shop and should have them with you whenever you are taking the dog out where he might foul a public place.

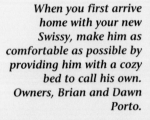

When you first arrive home with your new Swissy, make him as comfortable as possible by providing him with a cozy bed to call his own. Owners, Brian and Dawn Porto.

Your journey home should be made as quickly as possible. If it is a hot day, be sure the car interior is amply supplied with fresh air. It should never be too hot or too cold for the puppy. The pup must never be placed where he might be subject to a draft. If the journey requires an overnight stop at a motel, be aware that other guests will not appreciate a puppy crying half the night. You must regard the puppy as a baby and comfort him so he does not cry for long periods. The worst thing you can do is to shout at or smack him. This will mean your relationship is off to a really bad start. You wouldn't smack a baby, and your puppy is still very much just this.

ON ARRIVING HOME

By the time you arrive home the puppy may be very tired, in which case he should be taken to his sleeping

Your pup may be tired from his journey to his new home, so limit visitors and allow him plenty of time to become accustomed to his new surroundings. Owners, the Kleeman family.

area and allowed to rest. Children should not be allowed to interfere with the pup when he is sleeping. If the pup is not tired, he can be allowed to investigate his new home—but always under your close supervision. After a short look around, the puppy will no doubt appreciate a light meal and a drink of water. Do not overfeed him at his first meal because he will be in an excited state and more likely to be sick.

Although it is an obvious temptation, you should not invite friends and neighbors around to see the new arrival until he has had at least 48 hours in which to settle down. Indeed, if you can delay this longer then do so, especially if the puppy is not fully vaccinated. At the very least, the visitors might introduce some local bacteria on their clothing that the puppy is not immune to. This aspect is always a risk when a pup has been moved some distance, so the fewer people the pup meets in the first week or so the better.

DANGERS IN THE HOME

Your home holds many potential dangers for a little mischievous puppy, so you must think about these in advance and be sure he is protected from them. The more obvious are as follows:

Open Fires. All open fires should be protected by a mesh screen guard so there is no danger of the pup being burned by spitting pieces of coal or wood.

Electrical Wires. Puppies just love chewing on things, so be sure that all electrical appliances are neatly hidden from view and are not left plugged in when not in use. It is not sufficient simply to turn the plug switch to the off position—pull the plug from the socket.

Open Doors. A door would seem a pretty innocuous object, yet with a strong draft it could kill or injure a puppy easily if it is slammed shut. Always ensure there is no risk of this happening. It is most likely during warm weather when you have windows or outside doors open and a sudden gust of wind blows through.

Balconies. If you live in a high-rise building, obviously the pup must be protected from falling. Be sure he cannot get through any railings on your patio, balcony, or deck.

Ponds and Pools. A garden pond or a swimming pool is a very dangerous place for a little puppy to be near. Be sure it is well screened so there is no risk of the pup falling in. It takes barely a minute for a pup—or a child—to drown.

The Kitchen. While many puppies will be kept in the kitchen, at least while they are toddlers and not able to control their bowel movements, this is a room full of danger—especially while you are cooking. When cooking, keep the puppy in a play pen or in another room where he is safely out of harm's way. Alternatively, if you have a carry box or crate, put him in this so he can still see you but is well protected.

A pool can be a very dangerous place for a small puppy, so make sure your Swissy is closely supervised around water. Jimmy and Annie Barton with Ch. Allegro of High Ridge.

Be aware, when using washing machines, that more than one puppy has clambered in and decided to have a nap and received a wash instead! If you leave the washing machine door open and leave the room for any reason, then be sure to check inside the machine before you close the door and switch on.

Small Children. Toddlers and small children should never be left unsupervised with puppies. In spite of such advice it is amazing just how many people not only do this but also allow children to pull and maul pups. They

should be taught from the outset that a puppy is not a plaything to be dragged about the home—and they should be promptly scolded if they disobey.

Children must be shown how to lift a puppy so it is safe. Failure by you to correctly educate your children about dogs could one day result in their getting a very nasty bite or scratch. When a puppy is lifted, his weight must always be supported. To lift the pup, first place your right hand under his chest. Next, secure the pup by using your left hand to hold his neck. Now you can lift him and bring him close to your chest. Never lift a pup by his ears and, while he can be lifted by the scruff of his neck where the fur is loose, there is no reason ever to do this, so don't.

Puppies are naturally inquisitive and need to be watched closely to avoid getting into any kind of trouble. Barton Manor's Lady Guinivere owned by Donald and Diane Camp.

The first few nights away from his littermates may be lonely for your Swissy so give him plenty of attention and safe toys to keep him occupied. Shamrock Unforgettable owned by Katie Carman.

Beyond the dangers already cited you may be able to think of other ones that are specific to your home—steep basement steps or the like. Go around your home and check out all potential problems—you'll be glad you did.

THE FIRST NIGHT

The first few nights a puppy spends away from his mother and littermates are quite traumatic for him. He will feel very lonely, maybe cold, and will certainly miss the heartbeat of his siblings when sleeping. To help overcome his loneliness it may help to place a clock next to his bed—one with a loud tick. This will in some way soothe him, as the clock ticks to a rhythm not dissimilar from a heart beat. A cuddly toy may also help in the first few weeks. A dim nightlight may provide some comfort to the puppy, because his eyes will not yet be fully able to see in the dark. The puppy may want to leave his bed for a drink or to relieve himself.

If the pup does whimper in the night, there are two things you should not do. One is to get up and chastise him, because he will not understand why you are shouting at him; and the other is to rush to comfort him every time he cries because he will quickly realize that if he wants you to come running all he needs to do is to holler loud enough!

Puppies can get into just about anything and Snowy Mountain Ashley owned by Joyce Kolkmann looks about ready to get going!

By all means give your puppy some extra attention on his first night, but after this quickly refrain from so doing. The pup will cry for a while but then settle down and go to sleep. Some pups are, of course, worse than others in this respect, so you must use balanced judgment in the matter. Many owners take their pups to bed with them, and there is certainly nothing wrong with this.

The pup will be no trouble in such cases. However, you should only do this if you intend to let this be a permanent arrangement, otherwise it is hardly fair to the puppy. If you have decided to have two puppies, then they will keep each other company and you will have few problems.

OTHER PETS

If you have other pets in the home then the puppy must be introduced to them under careful supervision. Puppies will get on just fine with any other pets—but you must make due allowance for the respective sizes of the pets concerned, and appreciate that your puppy has a rather playful nature. It would be very foolish to leave him with a young rabbit. The pup will want to play and might bite the bunny and get altogether too rough with it.

Kittens are more able to defend themselves from overly cheeky pups, who will get a quick scratch if they overstep the mark. The adult cat could obviously give the pup a very bad scratch, though generally cats will jump clear of pups and watch them from a suitable vantage point. Eventually they will meet at ground level where the cat will quickly hiss and box a puppy's ears. The pup will soon learn to respect an adult cat; thereafter they will probably develop into great friends as the pup matures into an adult dog.

Swissys are usually very friendly and accommodating and will get along with any pet as long as properly introduced. Nox owned by Colleen and Tim Darnell plays with his friend.

HOUSETRAINING

Undoubtedly, the first form of training your puppy will undergo is in respect to his toilet habits. To achieve this you can use either newspaper, or a large litter tray filled with soil or lined with newspaper. A puppy cannot control

his bowels until he is a few months old, and not fully until he is an adult. Therefore you must anticipate his needs and be prepared for a few accidents. The prime times a pup will urinate and defecate are shortly after he wakes up from a sleep, shortly after he has eaten, and after he has been playing awhile. He will usually whimper and start searching the room for a suitable place. You must quickly pick him up and place him on the newspaper or in the litter tray. Hold him in position gently but firmly. He might jump out of the box without doing anything on the

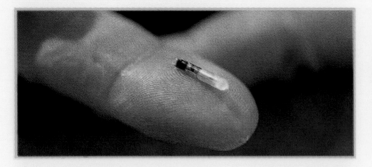

The newest method of identification is the microchip, a computer chip that is no bigger than a grain of rice, that is injected into the dog's skin.

first one or two occasions, but if you simply repeat the procedure every time you think he wants to relieve himself then eventually he will get the message.

When he does defecate as required, give him plenty of praise, telling him what a good puppy he is. The litter tray or newspaper must, of course, be cleaned or replaced after each use—puppies do not like using a dirty toilet any more than you do. The pup's toilet can be placed near the kitchen door and as he gets older the tray can be placed outside while the door is open. The pup will then start to use it while he is outside. From that time on, it is easy to get the pup to use a given area of the yard.

Many breeders recommend the popular alternative of crate training. Upon bringing the pup home, introduce him to his crate. The open wire crate is the best choice, placed in a restricted, draft-free area of the home. Put the pup's Nylabone® and other favorite toys in the crate along with a wool blanket or other suitable bedding. The puppy's natural cleanliness instincts prohibit him from soiling in the place where he sleeps, his crate. The puppy should be allowed to go in and out of the open crate during the day, but he should sleep in the crate at the night and at other intervals during the day. Whenever the pup is taken out of his crate, he should be brought outside (or to his newspapers) to do his business. Never use the crate as a place of punishment. You will see how quickly your pup takes to his crate, considering it as his own safe haven from the big world around him.

THE EARLY DAYS

You will no doubt be given much advice on how to bring up your puppy. This will come from dog-owning friends, neighbors, and through articles and books you may read on the subject. Some of the advice will be sound, some will be nothing short of rubbish. What you should do above all else is to keep an open mind and let common sense prevail over prejudice and worn-out ideas that have been handed down over the centuries. There is no one way that is superior to all others, no more than there is no one dog that is exactly a replica of another. Each is an individual and must always be regarded as such.

A dog never becomes disobedient, unruly, or a menace to society without the full consent of his owner. Your puppy may have many limitations, but the singular biggest limitation he is confronted with in so many instances is his owner's inability to understand his needs and how to cope with them.

IDENTIFICATION

It is a sad reflection on our society that the number of dogs and cats stolen every year runs into many thousands. To these can be added the number that get lost. If you do not want your cherished pet to be lost or stolen, then you should see that he is carrying a permanent identification number, as well as a temporary tag on his collar.

Permanent markings come in the form of tattoos placed either inside the pup's ear flap, or on the inner side of a pup's upper rear leg. The number given is then recorded with one of the national registration companies.

Make sure your Greater Swiss wears a collar and tags at all times in case he becomes lost or separated from you. Owners, Glen and Lisa Simonsen.

Research laboratories will not purchase dogs carrying numbers as they realize these are clearly someone's pet, and not abandoned animals. As a result, thieves will normally abandon dogs so marked and this at least gives the dog a chance to be taken to the police or the dog pound, when the number can be traced and the dog reunited with its family. The only problem with this method at this time is that there are a number of registration bodies, so it is not always apparent which one the dog is registered with (as you provide the actual number). However, each registration body is aware of his competitors and will normally be happy to supply their addresses. Those holding the dog can check out which one you are with. It is not a perfect system, but until such is developed it's the best available.

A temporary tag takes the form of a metal or plastic disk large enough for you to place the dog's name and your phone number on it—maybe even your address as well. In virtually all places you will be required to obtain a license for your puppy. This may not become applicable until the pup is six months old, but it might apply regardless of his age. Much depends upon the state within a country, or the country itself, so check with your veterinarian if the breeder has not already advised you on this.

For his safety and the safety of others, keep your Swissy on lead whenever you are out walking. Schaffhausen's Anticipation owned by Cilla Phillips and Tom Faber.

FEEDING YOUR GREATER SWISS MOUNTAIN DOG

Dog owners today are fortunate in that they live in an age when considerable cash has been invested in the study of canine nutritional requirements. This means dog food manufacturers are very concerned about ensuring that their foods are of the best

Your Swissy's mother will make sure your pup's nutritional needs are filled when first born. Int.Ch. Courtney, CGC, owned by Norman and DeLena Christensen, and her litter.

quality. The result of all of their studies, apart from the food itself, is that dog owners are bombarded with advertisements telling them why they must purchase a given brand. The number of products available to you is unlimited, so it is hardly surprising to find that dogs in general suffer from obesity and an excess of vitamins, rather than the reverse. Be sure to feed age-appropriate food—puppy food up to one year of age, adult food thereafter. Generally breeders recommend dry food supplemented by canned, if needed.

FACTORS AFFECTING NUTRITIONAL NEEDS

Activity Level. A dog that lives in a country environment and is able to exercise for long periods of the day will need more food than the same breed of dog living in an apartment and given little exercise.

Quality of the Food. Obviously the quality of food will affect the quantity required by a puppy. If the nutritional content of a food is low then the puppy will need more of it than if a better quality food was fed.

Balance of Nutrients and Vitamins. Feeding a puppy the correct balance of nutrients is not easy because the average person is not able to measure out ratios of one to another, so it is a case of trying to see that nothing is in excess. However, only tests, or your veterinarian, can be the source of reliable advice.

Genetic and Biological Variation. Apart from all of the other considerations, it should be remembered that each puppy is an individual. His genetic make-up will influence not only his physical characteristics but also his metabolic efficiency. This being so, two pups from the same litter can vary quite a bit in the amount of food they need to perform the same function under the same conditions. If you consider the potential combinations of all of these factors then you will see that pups of a given breed could vary quite a bit in the amount of food they will need. Before discussing feeding quantities it is valuable to know at least a little about the composition of food and its role in the body.

POPpups™ are 100% edible and enhanced with dog-friendly ingredients like liver, cheese, spinach, chicken, carrots, or potatoes. They contain no salt, sugar, alcohol, plastic or preservatives. You can even microwave a POPpup™ to turn into a huge crackly treat.

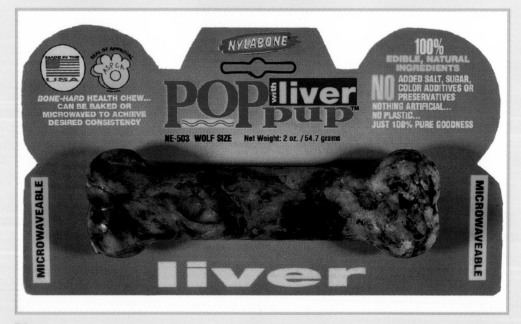

MADE WITH
REAL CARROTS

BONE-HARD
HEALTH CHEW
FIGHTS OBESITY AND
TOOTH PLAQUE

NYLABONE

Carrot
-BONE™

100% NATURAL
INGREDIENTS

NO ADDED SALT, SUGAR,
COLOR ADDITIVES OR
PRESERVATIVES

NCB-10z REGULAR SIZE
Net Weight: 1.1 oz. / 30 grams

Carrots are rich in fiber, carbohydrates, and vitamin A. The Carrot Bone™ by Nylabone® is a durable chew containing no plastics or artificial ingredients and it can be served as-is, in a bone-hard form, or microwaved to a biscuit consistency.

COMPOSITION AND ROLE OF FOOD

The main ingredients of food are protein, fats, and carbohydrates, each of which is needed in relatively large quantities when compared to the other needs of vitamins and minerals. The other vital ingredient of food is, of course, water. Although all foods obviously contain some of the basic ingredients needed for an animal to survive, they do not all contain the ingredients in the needed ratios or type. For example, there are many forms of protein, just as there are many types of carbohydrates. Both of these compounds are found in meat and in vegetable matter—but not all of those that are needed will be in one particular meat or vegetable. Plants, especially, do not contain certain amino acids that are required for the synthesis of certain proteins needed by dogs.

Likewise, vitamins are found in meats and vegetable matter, but vegetables are a richer source of most. Meat contains very little carbohydrates. Some vitamins can be synthesized by the dog, so do not need to be supplied via the food. Dogs are carnivores and this means their digestive tract has evolved to need a high quantity of meat as compared to humans. The digestive system of carnivores is unable to break down the tough cellulose walls of plant matter, but it is easily able to assimilate proteins from meat.

In order to gain its needed vegetable matter in a form that it can cope with, the carnivore eats all of its prey. This includes the partly digested food within the stomach. In commercially prepared foods, the cellulose is broken down by cooking. During this process the vitamin content is either greatly reduced or lost altogether. The manufacturer therefore adds vitamins once the heat process has been completed. This is why commercial foods are so useful as part of a feeding regimen, providing they are of good quality and from a company that has prepared the foods very carefully.

Proteins

These are made from amino acids, of which at least ten are essential if a puppy is to maintain healthy growth. Proteins provide the building blocks for the puppy's body. The richest sources are meat, fish and poultry, together with their by-products. The latter will include milk, cheese, yogurt, fishmeal, and eggs. Vegetable matter that has a high protein content includes soy beans, together with numerous corn and other plant extracts that have been dehydrated. The actual protein content needed in the diet will be determined both by the activity level of the dog and his age. The total protein need will also be influenced by the digestibility factor of the food given.

Fats

These serve numerous roles in the puppy's body. They provide insulation against the cold, and help buffer the organs from knocks and general activity shocks. They provide the richest source of energy,

Roar-Hide® is completely edible and is high in protein (over 86%) and low in fat (less than one-third of 1%). Unlike common rawhide, it is safer, less messy, and more fun.

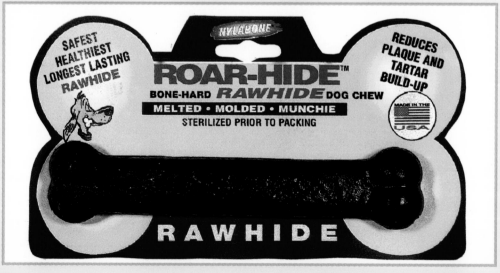

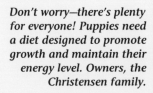

Don't worry—there's plenty for everyone! Puppies need a diet designed to promote growth and maintain their energy level. Owners, the Christensen family.

and reserves of this, and they are vital in the transport of vitamins and other nutrients, via the blood, to all other organs. Finally, it is the fat content within a diet that gives it palatability. It is important that the fat content of a diet should not be excessive. This is because the high energy content of fats (more than twice that of protein or carbohydrate) will increase the overall energy content of the diet. The puppy will adjust its food intake to that of its energy needs, which are obviously more easily met in a high-energy diet. This will mean that while the fats are providing the energy needs of the puppy, the over-all diet may not be providing its protein, vitamin, and mineral needs, so signs of protein deficiency will become apparent. Rich sources of fats are meat, their byproducts (butter, milk), and vegetable oils, such as safflower, olive, corn or soy bean.

Carbohydrates

These are the principal energy compounds given to puppies and adult dogs. Their inclusion within most commercial brand dog foods is for cost, rather than dietary needs. These compounds are more commonly known as sugars, and they are seen in simple or complex compounds of carbon, hydrogen, and oxygen. One of the simple sugars is called glucose, and it is vital to many metabolic processes. When large chains of glucose are created, they form compound sugars. One of these is called glycogen, and it is found in the cells of animals. Another, called starch, is the material that is found in the cells of plants.

Vitamins

These are not foods as such but chemical compounds that assist in all aspects of an animal's life. They help in so many ways that to attempt to describe these effectively would require a chapter in itself. Fruits are a rich source of vitamins, as is the liver of most animals. Many vitamins are unstable and easily destroyed by light, heat, moisture, or rancidity. An excess of vitamins, especially A and D, has been proven to be very harmful. Provided a puppy is receiving a balanced diet, it is most unlikely there will be a deficiency, whereas hypervitaminosis (an excess of vitamins) has become quite common due to owners and breeders feeding unneeded supplements. The only time you should feed extra vitamins to your puppy is if your veterinarian advises you to.

It's okay to give your dog treats on special occasions, but try not to upset his balanced diet. Barton Manor's Hugo owned by Brian and Dawn Porto.

Minerals

These provide strength to bone and cell tissue, as well as assist in many metabolic processes. Examples are calcium, phosphorous, copper, iron, magnesium, selenium, potassium, zinc, and sodium. The recommended amounts of all minerals in the diet has not been fully established. Calcium and phosphorous are known to be important, especially to puppies. They help in forming strong bone. As with vitamins, a mineral deficiency is most unlikely in pups given a good and varied diet. Again, an excess can create problems—this applying equally to calcium.

A complete and nutritionally balanced diet will be evident in your Swissy's shiny coat, healthy appearance and big smile! Shamrock Mecheck with his owners Greg and Kim Wotkop.

Water

This is the most important of all nutrients, as is easily shown by the fact that the adult dog is made up of about 60 percent water, the puppy containing an even higher percentage. Dogs must retain a water balance, which means that the total intake should be balanced by the total output. The intake comes either by direct input (the tap or its equivalent), plus water released when food is oxidized, known as metabolic water (remember that all foods contain the elements hydrogen and oxygen that recombine in the body to create water). A dog without adequate water will lose condition more rapidly than one depleted of food, a fact common to most animal species.

AMOUNT TO FEED

The best way to determine dietary requirements is by observing the puppy's general health and physical appearance. If he is well covered with flesh, shows good bone development and muscle, and is an active alert puppy, then his diet is fine. A puppy will consume about twice as much as an adult (of the same breed). You should ask the breeder of your puppy to show you the amounts fed to their pups and this will be a good starting point.

The puppy should eat his meal in about five to seven minutes. Any leftover food can be discarded or placed into the refrigerator until the next meal (but be sure it is thawed fully if your fridge is very cold).

When selecting a dog food for your Greater Swiss, make sure it provides adequate nutrition and is appropriate for his life stage. Ch. Shamrock Leader with owner Karen Conant.

If the puppy quickly devours its meal and is clearly still hungry, then you are not giving him enough food. If he eats readily but then begins to pick at it, or walks away leaving a quantity, then you are probably giving him too much food. Adjust this at the next meal and you will quickly begin to appreciate what the correct amount is. If, over a number of weeks, the pup starts to look fat, then he is obviously overeating; the reverse is true if he starts to look thin compared with others of the same breed.

WHEN TO FEED

It really does not matter what times of the day the puppy is fed, as long as he receives the needed quantity of food. Puppies from 8 weeks to 12 or 16 weeks need 3 or 4 meals a day. Older puppies and adult dogs should be fed twice a day. What is most important is that the feeding times are reasonably regular. They can be tailored to fit in with your own timetable—for example, 7 a.m. and 6 p.m. The dog will then expect his meals at these times each day. Keeping regular feeding times and feeding set amounts will help you monitor your puppy's or dog's health. If a dog that's normally enthusiastic about mealtimes and eats readily suddenly shows a lack of interest in food, you'll know something's not right.

TRAINING YOUR GREATER SWISS MOUNTAIN DOG

The process of training a Greater Swiss Mountain Dog might seem somewhat unusual in certain aspects when compared to other breeds. I've observed on my own and had many conversations with trainers locally, nationally and internationally who have noted these characteristics. I find it interesting that the observations have been the same for all of us but the interpretations of what is observed has varied to the extremes.

On one particular occasion, I had a conversation with a trainer of Search and Rescue dogs. He asked me straight away if whether Swissys were unusually quick learners who bored quickly in repetitive training sessions, or just slow to retain things. My response was an unqualified yes, that Swissys learn quickly as long as we are consistent in our training practices. He stated that he felt the same way, but since he had only seen one Swissy, he wanted to have verification of his evaluation.

Training your Greater Swiss takes time and patience, but you will eventually be rewarded with a well-behaved dog. Ryan Kleeman and Jingle take it one step at a time.

The Greater Swiss Mountain Dog is extremely trainable and eager to please and excels in all kinds of service work. Gunner and his German Shepherd friend are state police dogs.

Therefore, consistency on our parts can lead to a highly trained confident Greater Swiss Mountain Dog that will be the admiration of all who meet him.

Once your puppy has settled into your home and responds to his name, then you can begin his basic training. Before giving advice on how you should go about doing this, two important points should be made. You should train the puppy in isolation of any potential distractions, and you should keep all lessons very short. It is essential that you have the full attention of your puppy. This is not possible if there are other people about, or televisions and radios on, or other pets in the vicinity. Even when the pup has become a young adult, the maximum time you should allocate to a lesson is about 20 minutes. However, you can give the puppy more than one lesson a day, three being as many as are recommended, each well spaced apart.

Before beginning a lesson, always play a little game with the puppy so he is in an active state of mind and thus more receptive to the matter at hand. Likewise, always end a lesson with fun-time for the pup, and always—this is most important—end on a high note, praising the puppy. Let the lesson end when the pup has done as you require so he receives lots of fuss. This will really build his confidence.

COLLAR AND LEASH TRAINING

Training a puppy to his collar and leash is very easy. Place a collar on the puppy and, although he will initially try to bite at it, he will soon forget it, the more so if you play with him. You can leave the collar on for a few hours. Some people leave their dogs' collars on all of the time, others only when they are taking the dog out. If it is to be left on, purchase a narrow or round one so it does not mark the fur.

You can begin training your puppy as soon as he gets settled in his new home. Shamrock Unique, owned by Rob Waudby, at his graduation from puppy kindergarten.

Once the puppy ignores his collar, then you can attach the leash to it and let the puppy pull this along behind it for a few minutes. However, if the pup starts to chew at the leash, simply hold the leash but keep it slack and let the pup go where he wants. The idea is to let him get the feel of the leash, but not get in the habit of chewing it. Repeat this a couple of times a day for two days and the pup will get used to the leash without thinking that it will restrain him—which you will not have attempted to do yet.

Next, you can let the pup understand that the leash will restrict his movements. The first time he realizes this, he will pull and buck or just sit down. Immediately call the pup to you and give him lots of fuss. Never tug on the leash so the puppy is dragged along the floor, as this simply implants a negative thought in his mind.

Teaching your Swissy to walk on a leash is one of the easiest tasks you will undertake together. Black Creek's Abrams Tank owned by William Baldwin and Bunty Volls.

THE COME COMMAND

Come is the most vital of all commands and especially so for the independently minded dog. To teach the puppy to come, let him reach the end of a long lead, then give the command and his name, gently pulling him toward you at the same time. As soon as he associates the word come with the action of moving toward you, pull only when he does not respond immediately. As he starts to come, move back to make him learn that he must come from a distance as well as when he is close to you. Soon you may be able to practice without a leash, but if he is slow to come or notably disobedient, go to him and pull him toward you, repeating the command. Never scold a dog during this exercise—or any other exercise. Remember the trick is that the puppy must want to come to you. For the very independent dog, hand signals may work better than verbal commands.

THE SIT COMMAND

As with most basic commands, your puppy will learn this one in just a few lessons. You can give the puppy two lessons a day on the sit command but he will make just as much progress with one 15-minute lesson each day. Some trainers will advise you that you should not proceed to other commands until the previous one has been learned really well. However, a bright young pup is quite capable of handling more than one command per lesson, and certainly per day. Indeed, as time progresses, you will be going through each command as a matter of routine before a new one is attempted. This is so the puppy always starts, as well as ends, a lesson on a high note, having successfully completed something.

Call the puppy to you and fuss over him. Place one hand on his hindquarters and the other under his upper chest. Say "Sit" in a pleasant (never harsh) voice. At the same time, push down his rear end and push up under his chest. Now lavish praise on the puppy. Repeat this a few times and your pet will get the idea. Once the puppy is in the sit position you will release your hands. At first he will tend to get up, so immediately repeat the exercise. The lesson will end when the pup is in the sit position. When the puppy understands the command, and does it right away, you can slowly move backwards so that you are a few feet away from him. If he attempts to come to you, simply place him back in the original position and start again. Do not attempt to keep the pup in the sit position for too long. At this age, even a few seconds is a long while and you do not want him to get bored with lessons before he has even begun them.

THE HEEL COMMAND

All dogs should be able to walk nicely on a leash without their owners being involved in a tug-of-war. The heel command will follow leash training. Heel training is best done where you have a wall to one side of you. This will restrict the puppy's lateral movements, so you only have to contend with forward and backward situations. A fence is an alternative, or you can do the lesson in the garage. Again, it is better to do the lesson in private, not on a public sidewalk where there will be many distractions.

With a puppy, there will be no need to use a choke collar as you can be just as effective with a regular one. The leash should be of good length, certainly not too short. You can adjust the space between you, the

Snowy Mountain Beaureguard Zuger owned by Glen and Lisa Simonsen practicing the "heel."

puppy, and the wall so your pet has only a small amount of room to move sideways. This being so, he will either hang back or pull ahead—the latter is the more desirable state as it indicates a bold pup who is not frightened of you.

Hold the leash in your right hand and pass it through your left. As the puppy moves ahead and strains on the leash, give the leash a quick jerk backwards with your left hand, at the same time saying "Heel." The position you want the pup to be in is such that his chest is level with, or just behind, an imaginary line from your knee. When the puppy is in this position, praise him and begin walking again, and the whole exercise will be repeated. Once the puppy begins to get the message, you can use your left hand to pat the side of your knee so the pup is encouraged to keep close to your side.

It is useful to suddenly do an about-turn when the pup understands the basics. The puppy will now be behind you, so you can pat your knee and say "Heel." As soon as the pup is in the correct position, give him lots of praise. The puppy will now be beginning to associate certain words with certain actions. Whenever he is not in the heel position he will experience displeasure as you jerk the leash, but when he comes alongside you he will receive praise. Given these two

There's no telling how much you and your Swissy can accomplish! Here Ch. Barton Manor's Einstein, CGC owned by Colleen and Tim Darnell is winning Best of Breed.

Your Greater Swiss Mountain Dog must undergo basic obedience training if you wish to enter in dog shows together. Snowy Mountain Ashley owned by Joyce Kolkmann.

options, he will always prefer the latter—assuming he has no other reason to fear you, which would then create a dilemma in his mind.

Once the lesson has been well learned, then you can adjust your pace from a slow walk to a quick one and the puppy will come to adjust. The slow walk is always the more difficult for most puppies, as they are usually anxious to be on the move.

If you have no wall to walk against then things will be a little more difficult because the pup will tend to wander to his left. This means you need to give lateral jerks as well as bring the pup to your side. End the lesson when the pup is walking nicely beside you. Begin the lesson with a few sit commands (which he understands by now), so you're starting with success and praise. If your puppy is nervous on the leash, you should never drag him to your side as you may see so many other people do (who obviously didn't invest in a good book like you did!). If the pup sits down, call him to your side and give lots of praise. The pup must always come to you because he wants to. If he is dragged to your side he will see you doing the dragging—a big negative. When he races ahead he does not see you jerk the leash, so all he knows is that something restricted his movement and, once he was in a given position, you gave him lots of praise. This is using canine psychology to your advantage.

Always try to remember that if a dog must be disciplined, then try not to let him associate the discipline with you. This is not possible in all matters but, where it is, this is definitely to be preferred.

THE STAY COMMAND

This command follows from the sit. Face the puppy and say "Sit." Now step backwards, and as you do, say "Stay." Let the pup remain in the position for only a few seconds before calling him to you and giving lots of praise. Repeat this, but step further back. You do not need to shout at the puppy. Your pet is not deaf;

in fact, his hearing is far better than yours. Speak just loudly enough for the pup to hear, yet use a firm voice. You can stretch the word to form a "sta-a-a-y." If the pup gets up and comes to you simply lift him up, place him back in the original position, and start again. As the pup comes to understand the command, you can move further and further back.

The next test is to walk away after placing the pup. This will mean your back is to him, which will tempt him to follow you. Keep an eye over your shoulder, and the minute the pup starts to move, spin around and, using a sterner voice, say either "Sit" or "Stay." If the pup has gotten quite close to you, then, again, return him to the original position.

Always encourage your dog with praise and the occasional treat when he obeys your commands. Ch. Sennenhof's Ives owned by Julianne Wilson.

As the weeks go by you can increase the length of time the pup is left in the stay position—but two to three minutes is quite long enough for a puppy. If your puppy drops into a lying position and is clearly more comfortable, there is nothing wrong with this. Likewise, your pup will want to face the direction in which you walked off. Some trainers will insist that the dog faces the direction he was placed in, regardless of whether you move off on his blind side. I have never believed in this sort of obedience because it has no practical benefit.

THE DOWN COMMAND

From the puppy's viewpoint, the down command can be one of the more difficult ones to accept. This is because the position is one taken up by a submissive dog in a wild pack situation. A timid dog will roll over—a natural gesture of submission. A bolder pup will want to get up, and might back off, not feeling he should have to submit to this command. He will feel that he is under attack from you and about to be punished—which is what would be the position in his natural environment. Once he comes to understand this is not the case, he will accept this unnatural position without any problem.

A timid dog will roll over as a natural gesture of submission, but Hugo looks like he just wants his tummy scratched! Owners, Brian and Dawn Porto.

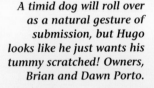

You may notice that some dogs will sit very quickly, but will respond to the down command more slowly—it is their way of saying that they will obey the command, but under protest!

There two ways to teach this command. One is, in my mind, more intimidating than the other, but it is up to you to decide which one works best for you. The first method is to stand in front of your puppy and bring him to the sit position, with his collar and leash on. Pass the leash under your left foot so that when you pull on it, the result is that the pup's neck is forced downwards. With your free left hand, push the pup's shoulders down while at the same time saying "Down." This is when a bold pup will instantly try to back off and wriggle in full protest. Hold the pup firmly by the shoulders so he stays in the position for a second or two, then tell him what a good dog he is and give him lots of praise. Repeat this only a few times in a lesson because otherwise the puppy will get bored and upset over this command. End with an easy command that brings back the pup's confidence.

The second method, and the one I prefer, is done as follows: Stand in front of the pup and then tell him to sit. Now kneel down, which is immediately far less intimidating to the puppy than to have you towering above him. Take each of his front legs and pull them forward, at the same time saying "Down." Release the legs and quickly apply light pressure on the shoulders with your left hand. Then, as quickly, say "Good boy" and give lots of fuss. Repeat two or three times only. The pup will learn over a few lessons. Remember, this is a very submissive act on the pup's behalf, so there is no need to rush matters.

RECALL TO HEEL COMMAND

When your puppy is coming to the heel position from an off-leash situation—such as if he has been running free—he should do this in the correct manner. He should pass behind you and take up his position and then sit. To teach this command, have the pup in front of you in the sit position with his collar and leash on. Hold the leash in your right hand. Give him the command to heel, and pat your left knee. As the pup starts to move forward, use your right hand to guide him behind you. If need be you can hold his collar and walk the dog around the back of you to the desired position. You will need to repeat this a few times until the dog understands what is wanted.

When he has done this a number of times, you can try it without the collar and leash. If the pup comes up toward your left side, then bring him to the sit position in front of you, hold his collar and walk him around the back of you. He will eventually understand and automatically pass around your back each time. If the dog is already behind you when you recall him, then he should automatically come to your left side, which you will be patting with your hand.

THE NO COMMAND

This is a command that must be obeyed every time without fail. There are no halfway stages, he must be 100-percent reliable. Most delinquent dogs have never been taught this command; included in these are the jumpers, the barkers, and the biters. Were your puppy to approach a poisonous snake or any other potential danger, the no command, coupled with the recall, could save his life. You do not need to give a specific lesson for this command because it will crop up time and again in day-to-day life.

A beautiful well-trained group of Greater Swiss! The Snowy Mountain gang at a dog show in Washington. Breeders, Norman and DeLena Christensen and Cathy Cooper.

If the puppy is chewing a slipper, you should approach the pup, take hold of the slipper, and say "No" in a stern voice. If he jumps onto the furniture, lift him off and say "No" and place him gently on the floor. You must be consistent in the use of the command and apply it every time he is doing something you do not want him to do.

HARNESS TRAINING

I've read about and talked with many breeders and trainers of other breeds who suggest that harness training can begin as early as six months of age. I strongly disagree with this practice for the Swissy. Because they are very slow to mature physically, this approach could seriously injure your growing Swissy.

In my opinion, intensive training for professional competition should not begin until the dog is two years old. Non-competitive training can begin at about 18

ISDRA Ch. IWPA Ch. Sennenhof's Mark owned by Jennifer Barton Demers competes in a weight pulling competition.

months of age in order for you and your dog to get in shape and just have fun. As with anything else, this depends on your dog's physical and mental maturity, health and willingness to pull. You should also perform a serious self evaluation to ensure your own commitment, because it will take a fair amount of time and expense for training and proper equipment. It isn't fair to your dog to partially prepare for carting or weight pulling. The result is often frustration for you and possible injury to your dog.

TEACHING YOUR SWISSY TO ACCEPT A HARNESS

There are a number of books available on types of harnesses, the correct fitting of the harness to your

To prevent injury to your Swissy, harness training should not begin until the dog is at least two years of age. Rosie and Belle practice carting around their young master.

dog, and methods on how to train your dog to accept wearing the harness. These books also discuss techniques for teaching your dog to pull a cart, wagon, sled, etc. Check out your local library or book store for titles.

You must *always* start off by introducing your dog to a cart harness. These harnesses have the least amount of material and supports hanging from them.

My personal approach with Swissys has been to simply make the event *not* an event. I just go about it as though it is a normal occurrence by playing with the dog and simply putting on the harness. At most, they try to smell the equipment, then readily accept it. This certainly suggests that your Swissy trusts you and knows that you would never do anything to hurt him. I have never had a Swissy show concern about wearing a harness right from the start.

COMPETITIVE WEIGHT PULLING AND CARTING

If you're interested in competitive weight pulling, get used to the snow and ice, because many of the competitions occur during the winter months, and brush up on your winter driving skills, you'll need them to get to many of the competitions.

The weight pulling competitions are nearly always held at interesting locations. For example, the Lake

George Weight Pull was held next to the fort where parts of the movie *The Last of the Mohicans* was filmed. Often, competitions are held in conjunction with sled dog races and winter carnivals at ski resorts or state parks.

When my daughter first introduced me to the idea of weight pulling, I argued against it thinking the worst. I did agree, however, to check it out in detail before committing to trying it out. I observed and learned how the pulls were organized and operated. Most importantly, I observed how the dogs were treated in training and in competition. In every case, I found all satisfactory.

The proper way to train your Greater Swiss for harness pulling is to slowly introduce him to the concept and keep it fun. Ch. Caesar and Ch. Elliot v Sarmac owned by Katie Carman play with some neighborhood kids.

The competition involves one dog harnessed to a large sled. This sled is to be pulled a set distance in a designated amount of time, depending on the rules of the hosting organization. The handler stands in front of his dog calling it forward. If the dog fails to reach him in the allotted time, the sled is pushed from behind without the dog's knowledge. This gives him the feeling of success that he was able to accomplish his task. If, however, the dog is successful on his own, he moves on to the next phase in the competition where more weight is added to the sled and he tries all over again. Ultimately, only one dog is successful in pulling the sled on his own, resulting in a win for that day's competition.

The dogs are not permitted to run and lunge from the sled against slackened harness lines. This is extremely dangerous and could easily result in injury to the dog. They are to start with taunt lines and just pull until either the sled crosses the finish line, time has run out, or the handler asks to have the sled pushed in order for the dog to accomplish his goal.

TEACHING YOUR SWISSY TO BEGIN PULLING

I've outlined several steps to help get you started in training and conditioning for both you and your dog.

1. Begin with muscle building and endurance — long walks up and down hills are preferable. Don't train in hot weather. *Do not feed your dog for several hours before or after training.*

2. Purchase a properly fitted weight pulling harness from a reputable dealer. Poor or improperly fitted equipment could possibly cause injury.

3. After a couple of weeks, you can begin training your dog to pull light weights. (At this point you'll need a friend to assist you in the training.) Fit the harness to your dog according to manufacturer instructions. Attach a car tire to the harness with a heavy duty rope capable of several thousand pounds tension. This rope must be securely fastened to the harness with a heavy duty quick release snap hook, also capable of tensions of several thousand pounds. Within a few months, your Swissy will be pulling such burdens. The tire should be about 10 feet behind your dog and should lay on its side. Have someone stand with your dog making certain he doesn't get tangled in the ropes. Also, have them keep tension on the line so that your dog doesn't lunge against the harness. You should then walk about 25 feet in front of your dog and call him to you with as much enthusiasm as you can muster. Again, so as to prevent injury to your dog, discourage your dog from backing up and lunging

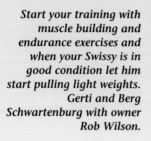

Start your training with muscle building and endurance exercises and when your Swissy is in good condition let him start pulling light weights. Gerti and Berg Schwartenburg with owner Rob Wilson.

against the harness and tires. Feet and legs can easily become entangled in loose lines and the dog might suffer severe injury to these limbs, as well as internal injuries if the chest bares full impact of the weight. When your dog reaches you, show him just how proud of him you are. **MAKE IT FUN!** Repeat this several times only. Watch your dog carefully, do not allow him to fatigue. You only need to practice three or four times each week.

4. Baiting your dog in competition is not permitted. Therefore practice the same way — do not use bait. Encourage your dog to pull for himself and you not for food.

5. After a couple of weeks, increase the weight by attaching two tires. **KEEP IT FUN!** Warm up with one tire, then add two.

6. If at any time you notice that your dog is disinterested or just not in the mood, **STOP**. If you notice that you aren't having a great day and that your temper is short, again stop. You can always train another day.

7. Keep up this process of practicing a few times each week with several pulls each time. Warm up with lighter weights, gradually increasing them. Don't start off with heavy weights and always have someone there to assist you.

8. Join a reputable national organization or affiliate in your area. If you are uncertain as to the reputation of an organization, contact your local Humane Society or the Greater Swiss Mountain Dog Club of America, Inc., for their assistance. Attend seminars and training programs. Go to the competitions with your dog and get pointers from the pros.

Combined with the natural physical capacity, the intelligence to quickly learn new tasks and the exceptional willingness to please, I have found most of our Swissys to be naturals at weight pulling and carting. I therefore find that it is unnecessary to adhere to rigid training programs with any of them. However, it is very important to keep your Swissy in top shape.

It is most unusual for any breed of dog to enter competition and become a medalist in his first year. Most often it takes a couple years of active competition before you can expect to beat the professionals.

Remember, these are generalizations of what I find helpful when working with my dogs. Modifications are always necessary in order to accommodate different dogs personalities, weather conditions and dog's abilities.

The competitive carting competitions are usually held throughout the year in less hostile weather conditions, and you and your Swissy will not be required to brave the elements in your travels and during the competition all the time. However, carting competitions may occasionally occur during summer months when high temperatures make it highly unfavorable for your Swissy. Therefore, I strenuously advise against carting and showing your Swissy during periods of high temperature.

Information on cart types, harness types, cart building and carting competitions is also available through the National Newfoundland Club and the National Bernese Mountain Dog Club. There are suppliers of sledding and carting equipment who also carry publications to help you get started.

The most important thing to remember if you decide to train your Swissy for harness pulling is to make it enjoyable for him. Owner, Jennifer Barton Demers.

YOUR HEALTHY GREATER SWISS MOUNTAIN DOG

Dogs, like all other animals, are capable of contracting problems and diseases that, in most cases, are easily avoided by sound husbandry—meaning well-bred and well-cared-for animals are less prone to developing diseases and problems than are carelessly bred and neglected animals. Your knowledge of how to avoid problems is far more valuable than all of the books and advice on how to cure them. Respectively, the only person you should listen to about treatment is your vet. Veterinarians don't have all the answers, but at least they are trained to analyze and treat illnesses, and are aware of the full implications of treatments. This does not mean a few old remedies aren't good standbys when all else fails, but in most cases modern science provides the best treatments for disease.

Opposite: Veterinarians are trained to analyze and treat illnesses. Having complete trust in your chosen veterinarian is tantamount to the long life of your dog.

PHYSICAL EXAMS

Your puppy should receive regular physical examinations or check-ups. These come in two forms. One is obviously performed by your vet, and the other is a day-to-day procedure that should be done by you. Apart from the fact the exam will highlight any problem at an early stage, it is an excellent way of socializing the pup to being handled.

To do the physical exam yourself, start at the head and work your way around the body. You are looking for any sign of lesions, or any indication of parasites on the pup. The most common parasites are fleas and ticks.

It is very important to brush your Swissy's teeth on a regular basis to fight tooth decay, periodontal disease and "doggy" breath. Hannibal gives his friend a great big kiss.

HEALTHY TEETH AND GUMS

Chewing is instinctual. Puppies chew so that their teeth and jaws grow strong and healthy as they develop. As the permanent teeth begin to emerge, it is painful and annoying to the puppy, and puppy owners must recognize that their new charges need something safe upon which to chew. Unfortunately, once the puppy's permanent teeth have emerged and settled solidly into the jaw, the chewing instinct does not fade. Adult dogs instinctively need to clean their teeth, massage their gums, and exercise their jaws through chewing.

It is necessary for your dog to have clean teeth. You should take your dog to the veterinarian at least once a year to have his teeth cleaned and to have his mouth examined for any sign of oral disease. Although dogs do not get cavities in the same way humans do, dogs'

The Hercules® by Nylabone® has raised dental tips that help fight plaque on your Greater Swiss Mountain Dog's teeth and gums.

teeth accumulate tartar, and more quickly than humans do! Veterinarians recommend brushing your dog's teeth daily. But who can find time to brush their dog's teeth daily? The accumulation of tartar and plaque on our dog's teeth when not removed can cause irritation and eventually erode the enamel and finally destroy the teeth. Advanced cases, while destroying the teeth, bring on gingivitis and periodontitis, two very serious conditions that can affect the dog's internal organs as well...to say nothing about bad breath!

Since everyone can't brush their dog's teeth daily or get to the veterinarian often enough for him to scale

Nylafloss® does wonders for your Greater Swiss Mountain Dog's dental health by massaging his gums and literally flossing between his teeth, loosening plaque and tartar build-up. Unlike cotton tug toys, Nylafloss® won't rot or fray.

the dog's teeth, providing the dog with something safe to chew on will help maintain oral hygeine. Chew devices from Nylabone® keep dogs' teeth clean, but they also provide an excellent resource for entertainment and relief of doggie tensions. Nylabone® products give your dog something to do for an hour or two every day and during that hour or two, your dog will be taking an active part in keeping his teeth and gums healthy...without even realizing it! That's invaluable to your dog, and valuable to you!

Nylabone® provides fun bones, challenging bones, and *safe* bones. It is an owner's responsibility to recognize safe chew toys from dangerous ones. Your dog will chew and devour anything you give him. Dogs must not be permitted to chew on items that they can break. Pieces of broken objects can do internal damage to a dog, besides ripping the dog's mouth. Cheap plastic or rubber toys can cause stoppage in the intestines; such stoppages are operable only if caught immediately.

The most obvious choices, in this case, may be the worst choice. Natural beef bones were not designed for chewing and cannot take too much pressure from the sides. Due to the abrasive nature of these bones, they should be offered most sparingly. Knuckle bones, though once very popular for dogs, can be easily

Nylabone® is the only plastic dog bone made of 100% virgin nylon, specially processed to create a tough, durable, completely safe bone.

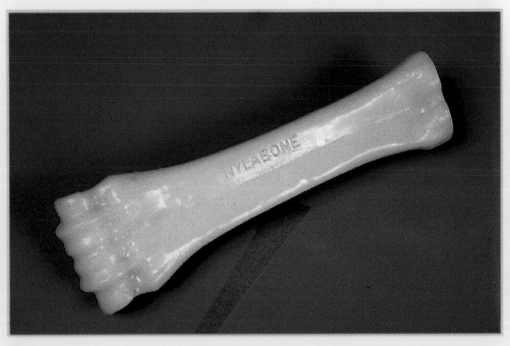

Chick-n-Cheez Chooz® are completely safe and nutritious health chews made from pure cheese protein, chicken, and fortified with vitamin E. They contain no salt, sugar, plastic, or preservatives and less than 1% fat.

chewed up and eaten by dogs. At the very least, digestion is interrupted; at worst, the dog can choke or suffer from intestinal blockage.

When a dog chews hard on a Nylabone®, little bristle-like projections appear on the surface of the bone. These help to clean the dog's teeth and add to the gum-massaging. Given the chemistry of the nylon, the bristle can pass through the dog's intestinal tract without effect. Since nylon is inert, no microorganism can grow on it, and it can be washed in soap and water or sterilized in boiling water or in an autoclave.

For the sake of your dog, his teeth and your own peace of mind, provide your dog with Nylabones®. They have 100 variations from which to choose.

FIGHTING FLEAS

Fleas are very mobile and may be red, black, or brown in color. The adults suck the blood of the host, while the larvae feed on the feces of the adults, which is rich in blood. Flea "dirt" may be seen on the pup as very tiny clusters of blackish specks that look like freshly ground pepper. The eggs of fleas may be laid on the puppy, though they are more commonly laid off the host in a favorable place, such as the bedding. They normally hatch in 4 to 21 days, depending on the temperature, but they can survive for up to 18 months if temperature conditions are not favorable. The larvae are maggot-like and molt a couple of times before forming pupae, which can survive long periods until the temperature, or the vibration of a nearby host, causes them to emerge and jump on a host.

There are a number of effective treatments available, and you should discuss them with your veterinarian, then follow all instructions for the one you choose. Any treatment will involve a product for your puppy or dog and one for the environment, and will require diligence on your part to treat all areas and thoroughly clean your home and yard until the infestation is eradicated.

THE TROUBLE WITH TICKS

Ticks are arthropods of the spider family, which means they have eight legs (though the larvae have six). They bury their headparts into the host and gorge on its blood. They are easily seen as small grain-like creatures sticking out from the skin. They are often picked up when dogs play in fields, but may also arrive in your yard via wild animals—even birds—or stray cats and dogs. Some ticks are species-specific, others are more adaptable and will host on many species.

The cat flea is the most common flea of dogs. It starts feeding soon after it makes contact with the dog.

The deer tick is the most common carrier of Lyme disease. Photo courtesy of Virbac Laboratories, Inc., Fort Worth, Texas.

The most troublesome type of tick is the deer tick, which spreads the deadly Lyme disease that can cripple a dog (or a person). Deer ticks are tiny and very hard to detect. Often, by the time they're big enough to notice, they've been feeding on the dog for a few days—long enough to do their damage. Lyme disease was named for the area of the United States in which it was first detected—Lyme, Connecticut—but has now been diagnosed in almost all parts of the U.S. Your veterinarian can advise you of the danger to your dog(s) in your area, and may suggest your dog be vaccinated for Lyme. Always go over your dog with a fine-toothed flea comb when you come in from walking through any area that may harbor deer ticks, and if your dog is acting unusually sluggish or sore, seek veterinary advice.

Attempts to pull a tick free will invariably leave the headpart in the pup, where it will die and cause an infected wound or abscess. The best way to remove ticks is to dab a strong saline solution, iodine, or alcohol on them. This will numb them, causing them to loosen their hold, at which time they can be removed with forceps. The wound can then be cleaned and covered with an antiseptic ointment. If ticks are common in your area, consult with your vet for a suitable pesticide to be used in kennels, on bedding, and on the puppy or dog.

INSECTS AND OTHER OUTDOOR DANGERS

There are many biting insects, such as mosquitoes, that can cause discomfort to a puppy. Many diseases are transmitted by the males of these species.

A pup can easily get a grass seed or thorn lodged between his pads or in the folds of his ears. These may go unnoticed until an abscess forms.

This is where your daily check of the puppy or dog will do a world of good. If your puppy has been playing in long grass or places where there may be thorns, pine needles, wild animals, or parasites, the check-up is a wise precaution.

SKIN DISORDERS

Apart from problems associated with lesions created by biting pests, a puppy may fall foul to a number of other skin disorders. Examples are ringworm, mange, and eczema. Ringworm is not caused by a worm, but is a fungal infection. It manifests itself as a sore-looking bald circle. If your puppy should have any form of bald patches, let your veterinarian check him over; a microscopic examination can confirm the condition. Many old remedies for ringworm exist, such as iodine, carbolic acid, formalin, and other tinctures, but modern drugs are superior.

There are many dangers in the great outdoors that your dog can encounter, so closely supervise him when he is outside. However, this Swissy looks like he has made a friend. Owner, Paulette Spiering.

Fungal infections can be very difficult to treat, and even more difficult to eradicate, because of the spores. These can withstand most treatments, other than burning, which is the best thing to do with bedding once the condition has been confirmed.

Mange is a general term that can be applied to many skin conditions where the hair falls out and a flaky crust develops and falls away.

Often, dogs will scratch themselves, and this invariably is worse than the original condition, for it opens lesions that are then subject to viral, fungal, or parasitic attack. The cause of the problem can be various species of mites. These either live on skin debris and the hair follicles, which they destroy, or they bury themselves just beneath the skin and feed on the tissue. Applying general remedies from pet stores is not recommended because it is essential to identify the type of mange before a specific treatment is effective.

Eczema is another non-specific term applied to many skin disorders. The condition can be brought about in many ways. Sunburn, chemicals, allergies to foods, drugs, pollens, and even stress can all produce a deterioration of the skin and coat. Given the range of causal factors, treatment can be difficult because the problem is one of identification. It is a case of taking each possibility at a time and trying to correctly diagnose the matter. If the cause is of a dietary nature then you must remove one item at a time in order to find out if the dog is allergic to a given food. It could, of course, be the lack of a nutrient that is the problem, so if the condition persists, you should consult your veterinarian.

INTERNAL DISORDERS

It cannot be overstressed that it is very foolish to attempt to diagnose an internal disorder without the advice of a veterinarian. Take a relatively common problem such as diarrhea. It might be caused by nothing more serious than the puppy hogging a lot of food or eating something that it has never previously eaten. Conversely, it could be the first indication of a potentially fatal disease. It's up to your veterinarian to make the correct diagnosis.

The following symptoms, especially if they accompany each other or are progressively added to earlier symptoms, mean you should visit the veterinarian right away:

Continual vomiting. All dogs vomit from time to time and this is not necessarily a sign of illness. They will eat grass to induce vomiting. It is a natural cleansing process common to many carnivores. However, continued vomiting is a clear sign of a problem. It may be a blockage in the pup's intestinal tract, it may be induced by worms, or it could be due to any number of diseases.

Diarrhea. This, too, may be nothing more than a temporary condition due to many factors. Even a change of home can induce diarrhea, because this often stresses the pup, and invariably there is some change in the diet. If it persists more than 48 hours then something is amiss. If blood is seen in the feces, waste no time at all in taking the dog to the vet.

Running eyes and/or nose. A pup might have a chill and this will cause the eyes and nose to weep. Again, this should quickly clear up if the puppy is placed in a warm environment and away from any drafts. If it does not, and especially if a mucous discharge is seen, then the pup has an illness that must be diagnosed.

Coughing. Prolonged coughing is a sign of a problem, usually of a respiratory nature.

Wheezing. If the pup has difficulty breathing and makes a wheezing sound when breathing, then something is wrong.

Cries when attempting to defecate or urinate. This might only be a minor problem due to the hard state of the feces, but it could be more serious, especially if the pup cries when urinating.

Cries when touched. Obviously, if you do not handle a puppy with care he might yelp. However, if he cries even when lifted gently, then he has an internal problem that becomes apparent when pressure is applied to a given area of the body. Clearly, this must be diagnosed.

Refuses food. Generally, puppies and dogs are greedy creatures when it comes to feeding time. Some might be more fussy, but none should refuse more than one meal. If they go for a number of hours without showing any interest in their food, then something is not as it should be.

General listlessness. All puppies have their off days when they do not seem their usual cheeky, mischievous selves. If this condition persists for more than two days then there is little doubt of a problem. They may not show any of the signs listed, other than perhaps a reduced interest in their food. There are many diseases that can develop internally without displaying obvious clinical signs. Blood, fecal, and other tests are needed in order to identify the disorder before it reaches an advanced state that may not be treatable.

WORMS

There are many species of worms, and a number of these live in the tissues of dogs and most other animals. Many create no problem at all, so you are not even aware they exist. Others can be tolerated in small levels, but become a major problem if they number more than a few. The most common types seen in dogs are roundworms and tapeworms. While roundworms are the greater problem, tapeworms require an intermediate host so are more easily eradicated.

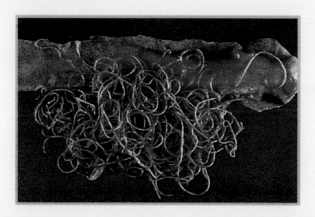

Roundworms are spaghetti-like worms that cause a pot-bellied appearance and dull coat, along with more severe symptoms, such as diarrhea and vomiting. Photo courtesy of Merck AgVet.

Roundworms of the species *Toxocara canis* infest the dog. They may grow to a length of 8 inches (20 cm) and look like strings of spaghetti. The worms feed on the digesting food in the pup's intestines. In chronic cases the puppy will become pot-bellied, have diarrhea, and will vomit. Eventually, he will stop eating, having passed through the stage when he always seems hungry. The worms lay eggs in the puppy and these pass out in his feces. They are then either ingested by the pup, or they are eaten by mice, rats, or beetles. These may then be eaten by the puppy and the life cycle is complete.

Larval worms can migrate to the womb of a pregnant bitch, or to her mammary glands, and this is how they pass to the puppy. The pregnant bitch can be wormed, which will help. The pups can, and should,

Whipworms are hard to find unless you strain your dog's feces, and this is best left to a veterinarian. Pictured here are adult whipworms.

be wormed when they are about two weeks old. Repeat worming every 10 to 14 days and the parasites should be removed. Worms can be extremely dangerous to young puppies, so you should be sure the pup is wormed as a matter of routine.

Tapeworms can be seen as tiny rice-like eggs sticking to the puppy's or dog's anus. They are less destructive, but still undesirable. The eggs are eaten by mice, fleas, rabbits, and other animals that serve as intermediate hosts. They develop into a larval stage and the host must be eaten by the dog in order to complete the chain. Your vet will supply a suitable remedy if tapeworms are seen or suspected. There are other worms, such as hookworms and

Just like new babies, young dogs receive immunity from their mothers for the first few months of life. A vaccination schedule should begin at six to eight weeks of age.

whipworms, that are also blood suckers. They will make a pup anemic, and blood might be seen in the feces, which can be examined by the vet to confirm their presence. Cleanliness in all matters is the best preventative measure for all worms.

Heartworm infestation in dogs is passed by mosquitoes but can be prevented by a monthly (or daily) treatment that is given orally. Talk to your vet about the risk of heartworm in your area.

VACCINATIONS

Every puppy, purebred or mixed breed, should be vaccinated against the major canine diseases. These are distemper, leptospirosis, hepatitis, and canine parvovirus. Your puppy may have received a temporary vaccination against distemper before you purchased him, but be sure to ask the breeder to be sure.

The age at which vaccinations are given can vary, but will usually be when the pup is 8 to 12 weeks old. By this time any protection given to the pup by antibodies received from his mother via her initial milk feeds will be losing their strength.

Rely on your veterinarian for the most effectual vaccination schedule for your Greater Swiss Mountain puppy.

The puppy's immune system works on the basis that the white blood cells engulf and render harmless

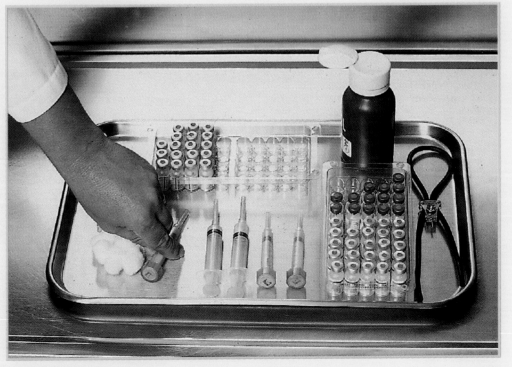

attacking bacteria. However, they must first recognize a potential enemy.

Vaccines are either dead bacteria or they are live, but in very small doses. Either type prompts the pup's defense system to attack them. When a large attack then comes (if it does), the immune system recognizes it and massive numbers of lymphocytes (white blood corpuscles) are mobilized to counter the attack. However, the ability of the cells to recognize these dangerous viruses can diminish over a period of time. It is therefore useful to provide annual reminders about the nature of the enemy. This is done by means of booster injections that keep the immune system on its alert. Immunization is not 100-percent guaranteed to be successful, but is very close. Certainly it is better than giving the puppy no protection.

Dogs are subject to other viral attacks, and if these are of a high-risk factor in your area, then your vet will suggest you have the puppy vaccinated against these as well.

Your puppy or dog should also be vaccinated against the deadly rabies virus. In fact, in many places it is illegal for your dog not to be vaccinated. This is to protect your dog, your family, and the rest of the animal population from this deadly virus that infects the nervous system and causes dementia and death.

ACCIDENTS

All puppies will get their share of bumps and bruises due to the rather energetic way they play. These will usually heal themselves over a few days. Small cuts should be bathed with a suitable disinfectant and then smeared with an antiseptic ointment. If a cut looks more serious, then stem the flow of blood with a towel or makeshift tourniquet and rush the pup to the veterinarian. Never apply so much pressure to the wound that it might restrict the flow of blood to the limb.

In the case of burns you should apply cold water or an ice pack to the surface. If the burn was due to a chemical, then this must be washed away with copious amounts of water. Apply petroleum jelly, or any vegetable oil, to the burn. Trim away the hair if need be. Wrap the dog in a blanket and rush him to the vet. The pup may go into shock, depending on the severity of the burn, and this will result in a lowered blood pressure, which is dangerous and the reason the pup must receive immediate veterinary attention.

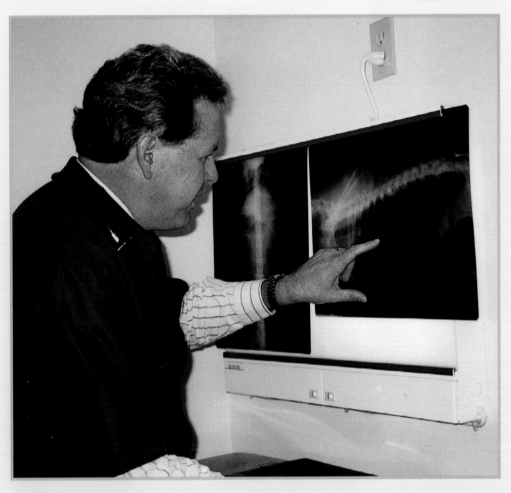

It is a good idea to x-ray the chest and abdomen on any dog hit by a car.

If a broken limb is suspected then try to keep the animal as still as possible. Wrap your pup or dog in a blanket to restrict movement and get him to the veterinarian as soon as possible. Do not move the dog's head so it is tilting backward, as this might result in blood entering the lungs.

Do not let your pup jump up and down from heights, as this can cause considerable shock to the joints. Like all youngsters, puppies do not know when enough is enough, so you must do all their thinking for them.

Provided you apply strict hygiene to all aspects of raising your puppy, and you make daily checks on his physical state, you have done as much as you can to safeguard him during his most vulnerable period. Routine visits to your veterinarian are also recommended, especially while the puppy is under one year of age. The vet may notice something that did not seem important to you.

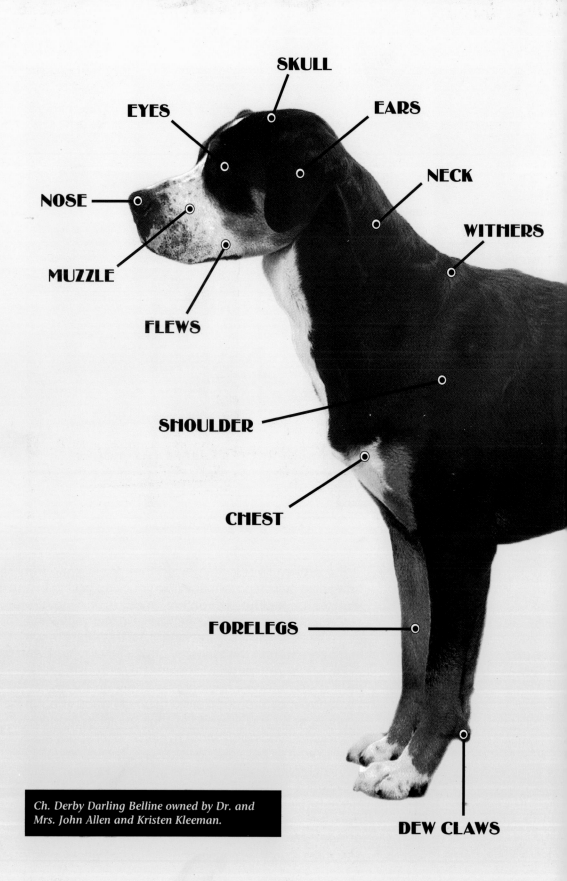

SKULL

EYES

EARS

NECK

NOSE

WITHERS

MUZZLE

FLEWS

SHOULDER

CHEST

FORELEGS

DEW CLAWS

Ch. Derby Darling Belline owned by Dr. and Mrs. John Allen and Kristen Kleeman.